Open Innovation Works

Successfully Leveraging Your External Ecosystem for Impactful Change

Diana Joseph
Dan Toma
Esther Gons

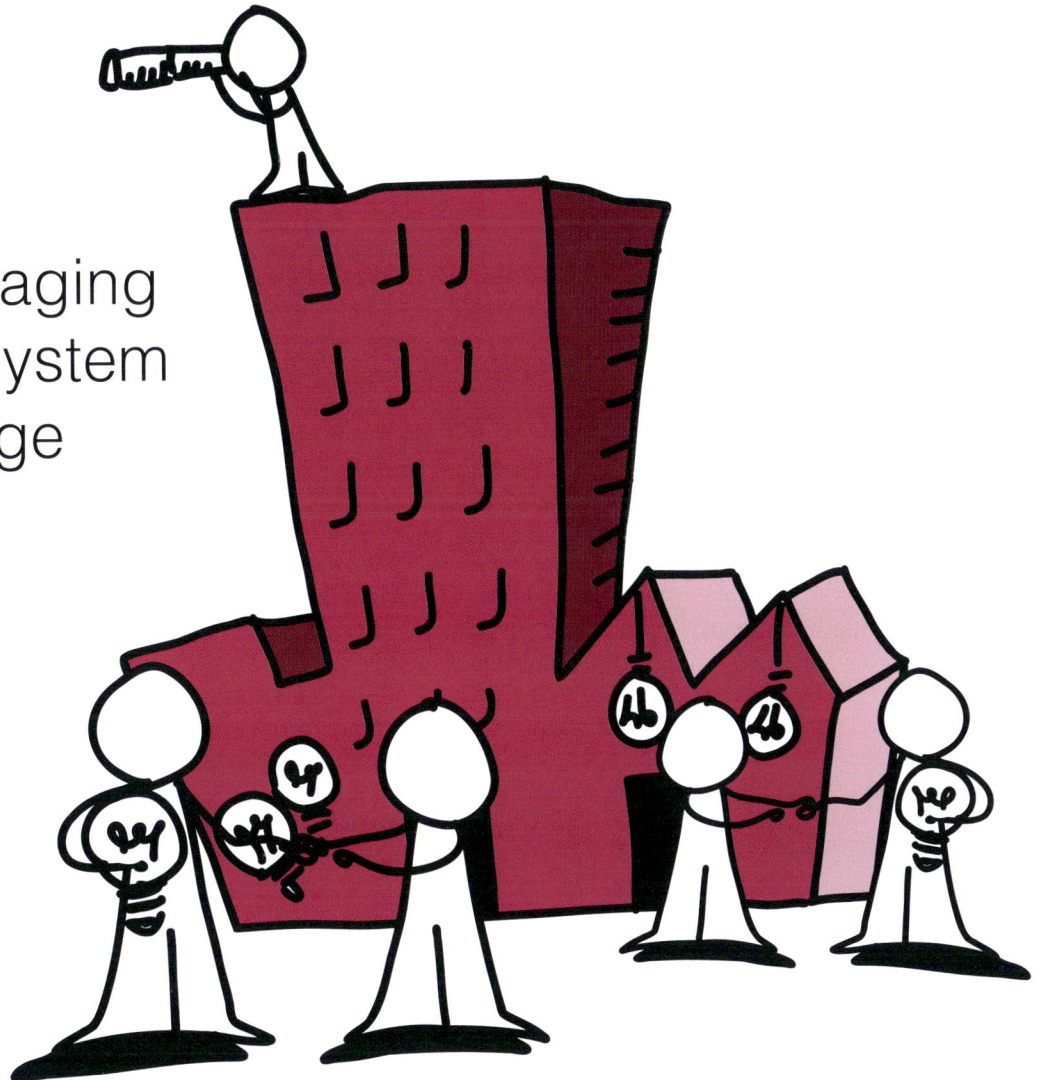

Open Innovation Works

Cover design, book design and illustrations:
Esther Gons, NEXT.amsterdam

Graphic execution:
Jorine Zegwaard, jorinezegwaard.nl

www.dianajoseph.com
www.danto.ma
www.estheremmelygons.nl
www.openinnovation.works

Emerald Publishing Limited

Emerald Publishing, Floor 5, Northspring, 21-23 Wellington Street,
Leeds LS1 4DL.

First edition 2026

Copyright © 2026 Diana Joseph, Dan Toma and Esther Gons
Published under exclusive licence by Emerald Publishing limited.

Reprints and permissions service
Contact: www.copyright.com

British Library Cataloguing in Publication Data
A catalogue record for this book is available from the British Library
Printed and bound in Great Britain by Bell and Bain Ltd, Glasgow
ISBN: 9781805920717 (Print)
ISBN: 9781805920687 (Online)
ISBN: 9781805920700 (Epub)

Introduction

Leading a large organization is a heavy responsibility. You've got thousands, or tens of thousands, or hundreds of thousands of mouths to feed. Stock exchanges and share owners demand good news followed by better news, quarter after quarter after quarter. Customers want higher and higher quality at lower and lower cost. On top of those direct stakeholders, there's also this: Large organizations own, or are, the infrastructure for everything that matters. If any desirable change is going to happen at scale (e.g., carbon reduction, fair labor practices, energy access, anything), large organizations have to be part of it—that's what scale is.

Somehow, you have to solve for all of those needs within the limits placed by governments and by your own processes, all while navigating obstacles generated by internal politics, and finicky press, and acts of nature, and a blindingly fast rate of technological change.

Here's the good news: Other entities in your ecosystem have different responsibilities, different superpowers, and different capacities. You and your partners can leverage these differences to find better, faster paths forward on your collective goals.

We're here to add a whole new drawer to your toolbox: Open Innovation. Partners out there in the ecosystem are better suited to discover new technologies, experiment with new business models, and bring more human capacities forward. Open innovation allows large organizations to bring your superpowers to bear through partnership, as we move to a world that works.

5

Table of Contents

PART 1

Open Innovation Ecosystem

The Engines

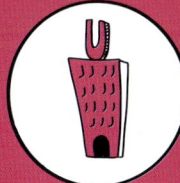

PART 1
Open Innovation Ecosystem

1
CHAPTER ONE

What Is Open Innovation and Why Does it Matter?

What's your greatest hope for your firm? Impact? Longevity? Profit?

Large firms are designed for maximum efficiency and stability. A corporation is a huge vessel—like a cruise ship or an aircraft carrier. It's meant to stay afloat, come what may, with a minimum of effort. One trade-off is that it's hard to steer. It's pretty good in a normal storm, but if something unexpected happens, there's very little the captain can do. And unexpected events are inevitable: The sheer size of the ship makes it impossible for the captain to stay aware of everything that's happening in front of the bow, behind the stern, to port and to starboard, above, below, and inside.

Do you remember Borders, the book and music megastore? The chain was a massive success in its time, an industry leader for thirty years before its collapse. Most of what you'll read on the Internet about Borders' demise points to bad, even foolish, decision-making on the part of Borders' executives—and it's true that Borders completely missed the boat on Internet commerce.

But put yourself in the shoes of Borders' leaders in the 1990s, pre-Amazon. You would have harbored reasonable skepticism about the importance of this trend: Is anyone really going to put their precious credit card data online? Are people really going to buy books without being able to pick them up, feel their weight, stroke the table of contents, flip through the illustrations? Do people really not care at all about the delicious experience of browsing favorite genres for hours, surrounded by books and booklovers? At that time in history, the *future* of the Internet was genuinely uncertain, and the *present* of the book megastore was strong.

How did a perfectly reasonable set of decisions result in bankruptcy?

When the world changed, Borders took what appeared to be the safer route—they stuck to what they knew in the short run, and when a significant alteration in the business environment arose, they joined it using a low-cost, fast-follower approach. The very desire for safety caused Borders executives to turn a blind eye to the future and entirely miss the opportunity to learn about the coming world of e-commerce.

We draw two important lessons from the Borders' tragedy (in classic Shakespearean terms, a story in which the protagonist causes their own demise):

1. Comfort is not the same as safety. Staying the course feels comfy because, by definition, you already have the relevant capacities in place to do what you're already doing. But with an uncertain future unfolding ahead of you, there's *no way to know* how long staying the course will work. Maybe it's already not working. Sticking to the well-lit spaces is a risky bet. You must hedge by placing some small bets in uncertain spaces.

2. Outsourcing is not innovation. When you partner as a way to explore the future, you must get more out of the deal than profit, products, and services. At least one central goal should always be *insight*. Who learned about e-commerce from the Borders–Amazon partnership? Clearly not Borders!

As e-retail became a reality and it was clearly time to engage, wouldn't it have seemed reasonable to outsource this newfangled function to a leading vendor, as Borders did with Amazon,[1] in the early 2000s? After all, you're a bookstore, not a tech company. Spending huge amounts of capital to become a tech company would have entailed taking on enormous, seemingly unnecessary, risk. Outsourcing to Amazon must have felt like a perfectly reasonable way to enter the online sales market.

Borders was a deeply customer-focused company in its bones,[2] with a solid track record of internal innovation. Their entire infrastructure was keyed to customer awareness in the megastore space. In a rapidly changing environment, wouldn't it have seemed reasonable to double down on the core business so they could serve even more customers with their top-notch experience? After all, that strategy had *always been successful before.*

11

"Never Delegate Understanding"

- Ray and Charles Eames[3]

Partnership with other entities is a powerful way to gain insight while keeping investment low, as long as the partnership approach is carefully chosen and well managed. We're here to share everything we've learned about exploring the future through partnership, a practice known as open innovation. Read on to discover whether, why, and how your company needs to step out of its comfort zone and participate actively in the open innovation ecosystem so the right insights arrive on time to make a difference!

The Open Innovation Imperative

Given the pace of paradigm shifts in technologies and in markets alike, corporates have to invest now in their long-term health. No matter how stable and reliable your business model is today, there's no guarantee it will outlive the next crisis or the next surprising new way to build, buy, or solve. Staying the course is extremely risky, at least as risky as innovation.

Internal innovation alone won't get you out of this jam. Corporates can accomplish a lot of things via internal research and development (R&D), but they can't do everything that way—regulations, hierarchy, incentives, and blind spots make it impossible to investigate the future sufficiently via internal activities alone.

If you're new to open innovation, you might feel like a pioneer, but don't worry, you're in good company. More and more firms are taking open innovation seriously. Corporate venture capital (CVC) efforts, for example, have grown steadily since the 2008 Global Financial Crisis,[4] and only increased in their investment since the COVID-19 pandemic.[5] Furthermore, chances are that the world will increasingly call on large firms to address global challenges such as climate change. The associated policies and customer sentiment will fuel further open innovation efforts.

Henry Chesbrough, widely recognized as the father of open innovation theory, kicked off this area of study in the early 2000s.[6] Today, we're here to guide you in how to execute, in practice. This book is designed to help you set a toehold in the future through partnerships that are *productive*, *strategic*, and *cost-efficient*. Your chosen partners may be peer firms, universities, municipalities, or just about any other entity in the ecosystem. Given our particular background and expertise, we'll put some special emphasis on open innovation with startups as we go.

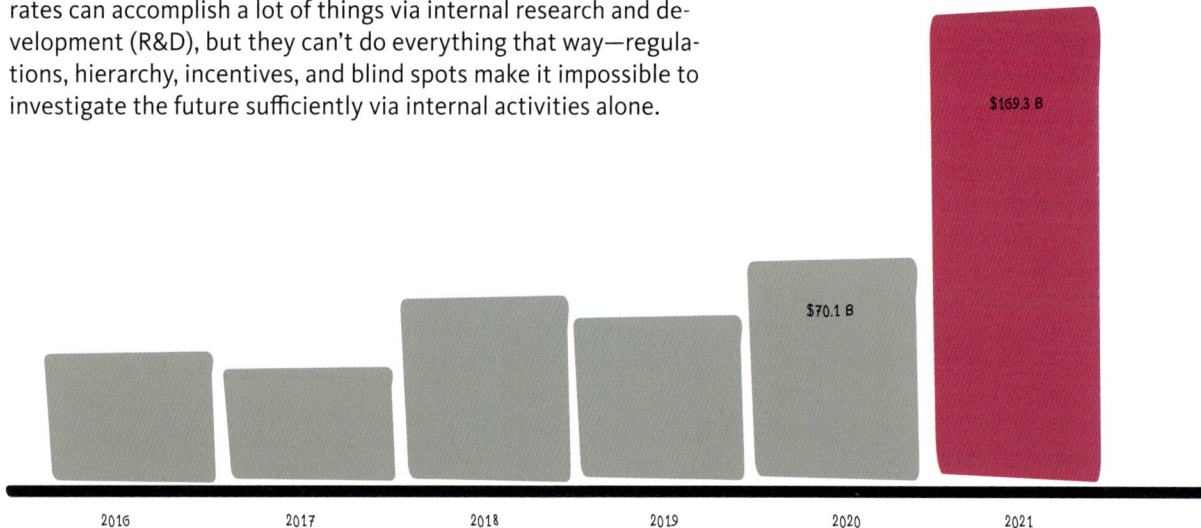

12

$169.3 B

$70.1 B

2016   2017   2018   2019   2020   2021

Corporate venture on the rise. PitchBook.

What Is Open Innovation?

We wrote in *The Corporate Startup* that innovation lies in the combination of great new ideas and profitable business models. Open innovation then can be defined as the practice of generating great new ideas and profitable business models *through partnership*. Sounds simple. Maybe it even feels like you're already doing it. Watch out though: You might be mistaking incremental novelty for innovation, and you might be mistaking simple purchasing for partnership.

When we speak of corporate open innovation, we mean that a large firm is engaging in a serious **partnership** with one or more other entities to learn, create, or deliver something **new**, beyond the boundaries of what the corporate can achieve on its own. We mean:

- there is **at least one other organizational party** at the table in addition to the corporate—such as a university, a startup, a nonprofit, or another large firm.
- it's a real **partnership**—both parties gain something, both parties contribute something, and the partnership generates something neither party could produce alone.
- it's intended to generate something manifestly **new** to these partners—an invention, business model, or knowledge that doesn't already exist.
- the corporate is doing this because it **can't be done, or can't be done well, by a large, highly aligned organization acting on its own**.

Chandrakant D. Patel of HP Inc.,
in an interview with Tolga Kortoglu[7] on open innovation:

"It is selfless. It is multidisciplinary. And the solutions matter to society."

Why Does Open Innovation Matter?

Corporates simply can't do all of the innovation they need with internal resources alone. While being inside a large firm conveys huge advantages, it also entails limitations. Putting it simply, the very corporate superpowers that account for the success of your core business put you in a bind when it comes to innovation.

THE INNOVATION BIND

Large firms have a bad reputation for breakthrough innovation—they're considered the stick-in-the-muds of the entrepreneurial ecosystem. Even inside of a large firm, folks with a penchant for change often perceive their colleagues as blockers. Why would otherwise smart and devoted people and organizations be so resistant to innovation? Large firms are bound to prioritize their core business, no matter how attractive the opportunity for innovation or how worrisome the winds of change. That's by design. Commitment to the core business isn't merely philosophical—it's structural. Frankly, large organizations are in a bind.

- *High alignment.* Corporates are large organizations designed to guide thousands, or tens or hundreds of thousands, of people in moving toward the same goal: profit. To get a huge group of people all to move in the same direction, large firms need to optimize alignment. They use structures like formal job requisitions, job descriptions, incentives, hierarchy, employee performance improvement mechanisms, and inorganic culture to ensure conformity to the corporate vision and goals. *These same mechanisms are precisely what you'd use if you purposely wanted to **prevent** breakthrough ideas from bearing fruit.*
- *Reporting requirements.* Public (listed) firms must report on a quarterly basis to shareholders and regulatory agencies which wield significant power to impact the firm's fortunes. Every quarterly analyst call is a new opportunity for Wall Street or its regional equivalent to strike at your stock price—miss a forecast and down goes the value of your firm and its executives. Quarterly goals constantly shove longer-term goals to the background. Furthermore, shareholder scrutiny

13

prevents movement of significant funds into explicit innovation activities due to concerns about being perceived as defunding the core.

- *Regulations.* In many places, large firms are held to a higher standard with regard to certain types of policies, for example, in the human resources domain. These standards bring important benefits to the broader social system, and at the same time, they add significant weight to decisions, reducing available cash and slowing down processes.
- *Information lock.* Large firms worry about strategy and intellectual property (IP) leakage and therefore sometimes prevent employees from engaging with external informants.
- *Brand lock.* Large firms invest millions in developing their brand and feel obliged to celebrate it, protect it, and use it. Attaching the brand to an exploratory project feels risky, but omitting the brand feels disingenuous and might even be illegal.
- *Effort lock.* The drive for efficiency means that every employee is meant to be fully booked at all times. For a salaried employee, there's no real limit to the number of hours the firm can demand. At firms like Google, where every employee is theoretically allotted 20% of their time to innovate, that often just means that they're invited to work 120% of their time. So, employees don't necessarily welcome or take advantage of innovation initiatives.

Alignment, profit maximization, and devotion to the core business can be healthy for large firms and their shareholders. However, these same values promote a narrow outlook, short-term investment, and constrained behavior. These patterns limit the extent to which large firms can engage with their customers and communities, explore, understand, and prepare for possible futures, usher in desired futures, or attempt to limit undesired futures.

So, what's the answer? Is it time to fling open the gates, set employees loose to do whatever they want, hide innovation activities, defy regulations, make all IP open source, and drop branding? Of course not!

Let's innovate!

You can get a lot done with internal innovation, we see it all the time. Inside the firm, corporates create space for employees to act like startups (see *The Corporate Startup*[8]) and to measure the effects appropriately (see *Innovation Accounting*[9]). Internal innovation can generate patents, inspire new products and services, and cement employee loyalty. But the concerns we've described create hard limits on engaging with the outside world, and therefore limits on vision. If you're not engaging with the outside world, you can't see the future coming. So, there are some crucial innovation spaces you're bound not to explore.

14

Note: If your main problem is that internal innovation is failing due to broken structure and strategy, shifting to open innovation won't help—your core problems will simply transfer to the open initiative and cause equal havoc in a more public setting.

WHEN YOU'RE IN A BIND, ENGAGE PARTNERS

When you see an improvement or exploration opportunity that can be completed exclusively with internal resources, you should definitely do that! Internal-only novelty can be cheaper, intellectual property considerations are clear, you get all the value if you're successful, and nobody knows if you fail. But the constraints we've described limit what's possible with internal resources only.

Look to open innovation when your organizational constraints block you from exploring a question on your own.

As a corporation you need to engage in open innovation to face challenges that you are *functionally blocked* from pursuing on your own because of the demands of internal alignment, regulation, or stakeholder limitations. For example:

- Questions that demand embedded observation of customer practice (cf. Illumina for Startups). The corporate simply can't get close enough to its customers to observe their environments and behaviors unless it truly partners with customers.
- Challenges that require high-speed motion (cf. Pfizer's partnership with BioNTech). Huge companies have massive processes and are notoriously hard to shift.
- Challenges that someone else is solving more effectively (cf. Google and Upstartle, the originator of Writely, which was the basis of Google Docs).
- Challenges that invite a major shift (cf. the travel company, TUI, and its acquisition of Musement).
- Ecosystem-level challenges (cf. Eastman, cf. automotive coalition). Some challenges, like the circular economy or self-driving cars, need to be solved by an entire ecosystem working together.

Partners can get you unstuck because they are optimized for different behaviors and different sensemaking. They have different histories, goals, constraints, structures, and cultures. Through partnership, you access their eyes on the future, their experiments, their speed, and their expertise while granting them access to your breadth of knowledge, expansive relationships, and capacity for scale. Through leading or participating in ecosystems, you take advantage of the synergies between multiple players.

15

Have a look at the strengths and corresponding needs of some of the entities in an entrepreneurial ecosystem:

Research universities develop new insight at the edge of what humanity already understands. They need partners to bring these insights into ordinary human experience.
-a view into the long-term future.

Startups explore and take advantage of the uncertainty of the future by making and testing things and experiences people might (or might not) want. Most of them need partners to navigate the steps required to achieve a broad impact.
-derisk the commercialization of new ideas.

Nonprofits/nongovernmental organizations (NGOs) fulfill a specific purpose on behalf of the public. They usually need funding partners, since their customers can't be their only source of revenue.
-solve important problems whose commercial value is invisible.

16

Governments deliver a functioning infrastructure. They often need partners[10] to extend their impact.
-maintain stability, deliver effective solutions to a broad populace.

Small businesses provide a repeatable answer to a known and stable need. They need partners to access knowledge and economies of scale.
-consistent, real-time delivery of a key local asset.

Large commercial firms deliver a body of products and services efficiently. They need partners to get ahead of coming changes.
-synergistic forward motion on a complex effort.

Each type of partner has different assets, and different capacity gaps, and different perspectives.

Driving Open Innovation

As we've said, open innovation can feel somewhat easier than internal innovation, because it shares effort and risk outside the firm. Even so, it's no small matter to unlock open innovation. You're asking a risk-averse organization to recognize that doing nothing is itself risky. You're asking to channel money, time, and effort in a new direction. Those resources are reallocated from somewhere, representing a loss to real people.

To make it work, you need internal allies to recognize the importance of the effort and sign on to contribute or, at minimum, not to interfere. To engage their alignment, invite the right stakeholders to codesign from the beginning so that the effort genuinely represents their interests. One piece of good news: Alignment is a superpower for large firms—you just need to point a bit of your alignment practice in the open innovation direction.

So how are you actually going to do the work of getting aligned? And what are you going to align on? How does all that alignment produce open innovation? How does open innovation actually create important outcomes? Let's find out!

Exercise Do I Need This Book?

You've taken the first step—you've opened the book! You're about to invest serious time and treasure in making open innovation work for your company. Before diving in, let's find out why you need innovation, why open innovation in particular, and what capacity you have to take on this journey.

Rate yourself on a scale from 1–5 on each of these core questions. Then flip the page to find your score and recommendation about whether you should read on or not.

Remember: This is private. Answer honestly to get real feedback.

Does Our Firm Need Innovation?

QUESTION 1: EXPIRATION DATE. How much time remains in your most profitable business?

All businesses end. Predict the expiration date of your most profitable business. The expiration date is the moment where your growth curve swings down. (To learn more about expiration dates, see our prior book, *Innovation Accounting*[9], Chapter 6.) Some factors to consider:

- *Is your **market** still growing? When is it likely to stop, that is, when will your sector have reached just about every consumer who will buy?*
- *Is your **share** of market growing? When will your higher-priced competitors be able to match your price? When will your lower-quality competitors be able to match your quality? You might use a Portfolio Fade calculation (see* Innovation Accounting*) to help you make sense of this. Chart your key offering's share of market over the last 1–5 years, and consider factors that might impact it over the next few years.*
- *Is anything happening in the market that could reduce the **importance** of the problem you solve? If so, when will the hit to your bottom line arrive? For example, in 2025, if you still make a part for internal combustion engines, you're paying close attention to regulations in California that may bring sales of internal combustion engines to an end in the next few years. If you make software for online meetings, your COVID-19 boom is over. If your supplies rely on international or even interstate chains, could there be a global disruption on its way?*

If your core business has a few years left, open innovation may be a powerful tool for you. If your business is going to last forever, maybe you can pass on open innovation. If your business is in emergency mode, you may be too late for open innovation, or any innovation practice for that matter, to be of much help.

We likely have this many growth years remaining in our most profitable business.

0–our most profitable business has already expired or will expire in the next year	2–4 years	5–7 years	8–10 years	>10 years remain
○ 1	○ 2	○ 3	○ 4	○ 5
				Are you sure? It's very hard to generate evidence for more than a decade of profitability at this time of great change. We suggest you recheck your evidence.

QUESTION 2: EXTERNAL PRESSURES. How might issues outside of your control impact your business?

Regardless of your general expiration date expectations, the outside world may shake things up.

- *Will **climate change** and unexpected weather impact your business dramatically (or have they already)?*
- *Has any **major global event**, such as a pandemic or a war, caused major disruption in your business? Could another geopolitical or environmental change easily cause more major disruption in your business?*
- *Does your business depend on a certain **regulatory framework**? Could regulatory change cause major disruption in your business (for example, changes to tariffs, taxes, data control measures, bans on dangerous materials or energy sources, etc.)? Could the easing of certain regulations disrupt your business (for example, if you are a tax preparation firm and the tax code is simplified, what will happen to your business? Or (remember this one?) if your firm distributes medical masks and they are no longer required, ...)?*
- *What happens to your business when a new **trend** arises? (Consider: artificial intelligence, blockchain, quantum computing. Did you/ do you ignore them? Scramble to follow? Or do you already have toeholds in those spaces?)*
- *Are you **prepared** for external events? Does your firm have effective plans in place to address disruption?*

If you have no interest in the possibility of disruption, you're not going to get much from open innovation. Otherwise, open innovation can provide a new lens into what might be coming, and how to encourage positive outcomes.
Here's where we are with regard to external pressures.

We try hard not to think about what could happen. One foot in front of the other.	We know external circumstances could have extreme effects on our business, but we don't have any particular plans to address them. We'll cross that bridge when we come to it.	We have preparations in place for external events that have already happened, so we're ready if they happen again—like a COVID-19 hospitalization spike or an earthquake in Taiwan. But if a new event occurs, we don't have a plan.	We have good plans in place, but it's not clear we would be able to execute them if something happened.	We consistently consider what low-probability, high-impact events might occur. We have specific plans to address the ones we're aware of, and we have a general strategy to prepare for surprises. We check these plans regularly and practice for events.
○ 1	○ 2	○ 3	○ 4	○ 5

Does Our Firm Need Open Innovation, Per Se?

QUESTION 3: FUNCTIONAL BLOCKAGE. Are you able to answer every innovation question you have through internal resources, or are certain important explorations forbidden?

FOR EXAMPLE:
- **Brand lock**: *Will your brand managers permit in-market experiments to go forward, marked with the official brand? Will regulations or internal policies permit you to remove your brand from in-market experiments?*
- **Financial risk**: *What level of financial risk is preapproved with your finance department and Board of Directors? Could you take a $100K risk on a commercial experiment without going through an approval process (or is the approval process quick)?*
- **Stakeholder sensitivity**: *Do your shareholders demand pure focus on the core business? Are quarterly reporting concerns driving all prioritization decisions?*
- **Culture**: *When an employee wants to spend time on an idea, how does their manager respond? What preset incentives encourage or discourage this behavior? For example, do employees benefit from the success of a specific business to which they contribute? On the other hand, do employees get huge bonuses to reward them for a laser focus on the core business? Are they reprimanded for spending time on something else?*

It will be very hard to investigate the future if you can't do an experiment with the brand, but you can't do an experiment without the brand; if staff are incentivized purely on existing job description, if internal budgets are strictly managed for the core. On the other hand, if everything is awesome, you may not need external partnership to explore.

Are we functionally blocked from pursuing certain types of critically important exploration projects?

No problem, we happily explore as needed using 100% internal resources, no need for outside partnership, whatsoever.	We have an inkling that internal innovation might not give us all the insight we need to prepare for the future, but we're not taking action right now.	We know that important change is happening beyond our walls, so we are watching and waiting.	We understand that functional, structural factors prevent our exploration in certain ways. We're not ready to take specific actions.	We're fully aware: There's a host of critical innovation questions we simply can't address on our own, and we're ready to explore externally.
Are you sure? It might be a good idea to consider whether you have some blind spots with regard to preparing for the future.	*This position is otherwise known as "learning the hard way."*			
○ 1	○ 2	○ 3	○ 4	○ 5

QUESTION 4: DOES THE OUTSIDE WORLD HAVE THE IDEAS, PERSPECTIVES, RESOURCES, SKILLS, AND/OR TALENT WE NEED?

Whether or not you have all the capacities you need internally, it's worth asking whether anyone in the outside world has them, and, if so, who? At minimum, you'll want ways to observe how those folks are engaging in the ecosystem, and perhaps you'll want to partner with them.

Considerations:
- *Are your **direct competitors** currently exploring new ideas that could disrupt your company or your industry? Or rather—your direct competitors are certainly exploring new ideas that could disrupt your company or industry. Do you know how? Are you also doing this kind of exploration?*
- *Are organizations and people in **other sectors** currently exploring concepts that could fundamentally change something important about how your business functions? Could the problem your core business currently solves disappear via the efforts of some other sector (for example: As electric mobility rises, the problem solved by spark plugs will disappear)? Are you also exploring how you might benefit from the eventual eradication of the problem you currently solve?*
- *Could you solve upcoming challenges through partnerships with **other giants** in adjacent or different industries? (Consider, for example, the robotics–AI–automotive consortium addressing self-driving cars in the 2020s https://www.avcconsortium.org/)*
- *Do you want an early view of **university** research?*
- *Are **startups** nimbly exploring arenas that are important to you, faster and with less restriction that you can manage?*

Values are what you demonstrate. If you do everything in-house, you likely don't truly value what's outside, so you're not ready for real partnership (yet). If you're starting to explore partnerships, great! If you're deeply engaged with external entities already, formalizing an open innovation practice could help you draw even more value.
What is the evidence that we believe in the value of external partnership?

We have very strong organizational boundaries. We are relying on the long-term value of our intellectual property (IP), and not paying too much attention to anyone else.	We're dabbling in external partnerships.	We know there's important activity happening in the outside world, and we participate in a formal way through activities like grants and sponsorships, but we aren't really engaging deeply with other entities.	We have some good active partnerships and a presence in the ecosystem, but we know we could play a bigger role.	We are deeply engaged in the external ecosystem of ideas—exchanging resources and efforts with other entities on a consistent basis.
○ 1	○ 2	○ 3	○ 4	○ 5

Do We Have the Capacity?

QUESTION 5: DOES YOUR COMPANY HAVE THE *MATURITY* TO ENGAGE IN OPEN INNOVATION?

- *Consider: Does your leadership have a strong hand on the wheel? Does your staff **trust leadership** to take the organization in a healthy direction? If your leaders were to announce a new open innovation engine, would rank-and-file employees respond with applause, or an eyeroll, or fear/anger?*
- *Consider: Are your **processes and culture in place** to allow open innovation efforts to move forward well? If an internal innovator found an external partner, could they bring it to internal stakeholders? Could those internal stakeholders take advantage of the opportunity? Could they make real changes based on what they learn? Could that happen in weeks or months vs. years or decades?*

To fully benefit from open innovation, you need to take it in. Are you ready to do that?
How ready are we to embrace outside ideas and partners?

Our company immediately rejects any new idea, due to structure, process, culture, or leadership.	We understand that open innovation requires mature processes, culture, and leadership, but we have not yet started to build these capabilities.	We have begun to build the leadership, process, and culture capabilities needed for open innovation.	Our maturity is solid and we are working to address some shortcomings in our capabilities that might currently be getting in the way of consistent open innovation results.	Our company is absolutely ready to take advantage of new ideas from outside—we can tell because we are already doing this and seeing impactful results.
○ 1	○ 2	○ 3	○ 4	○ 5

QUESTION 6: WHAT IS YOUR CAPACITY FOR INNOVATION IN GENERAL?

If *internal* innovation is failing at your company, *open* innovation may not work either. You'll need robust capacities, or a willingness to develop robust capacities, in either case. Consider:

- *Are you asking important innovation questions (yet)? That is,* **is innovation on your radar** *in the first place?*
- *What's your appetite for* **risk?** *Are experiments encouraged? Are interesting failures honored and treated as a source of learning? How does the organization respond to failures and mistakes, interesting or otherwise? How does the organization recognize the risk of doing nothing (e.g., the risk of coming too late to a change in the market, the risk of a competitor taking the industry in a new direction, etc.)?*
- *Does your internal research and development (R&D) department reliably drive the* **creation of new profitable businesses***? (R&D departments are often considered highly productive if they generate new patents. But most patents do not lead to new businesses.) When was the last time a profitable new product or service arose from internal efforts alone? If you are already consistently innovating in the sense that you're creating profitable new businesses on a regular basis, that's a good sign that you're ready to take advantage of open innovation as well.*
- *Do you have a reliable* **pathway for ideas from employees** *outside of R&D to reach the market? How many ideas per year, arising from internal employees, are tested for commercial possibilities? How many become major profitable new businesses? Again, if you already have mechanisms in place for ideas to become reality, you're likely ready for open innovation.*
- *Are you* **already engaging successfully** *in open innovation? For example: Do you have a scouting program that generates healthy partnerships that in turn lead to healthy new businesses? Do you have a robust university partnership program? An obvious door through which startups can reach you easily? Are you a lead voice in your regional and industry innovation ecosystems?*
- **Processes:** *How long does it take to get a new project approved for exploration? How long does it take to get a contract signed? A payment delivered?*
- *Do employees have designated* **time** *to explore the future? If an idea turns out to be interesting, can an internal employee draw on time from their colleagues without going through an approval process? Can an employee with an idea explore it on company time?*

Strong innovation muscles serve both internal and external innovation. If you're doing one well, the other will come fairly naturally.
What is the evidence for our innovation success?

We don't do innovation. (We may buy fully realized products and services to expand our offerings.)	We invent things but our track record for turning these inventions into businesses is weak.	We've created at least one thriving new business out of our innovation practice.	We have a few examples of turning ideas into new businesses over the past few years.	We consistently create new products, services, and businesses.
○ 1	○ 2	○ 3	○ 4	○ 5

QUESTION 7: DOES YOUR COMPANY HAVE THE *RESOURCES* TO ENGAGE IN OPEN INNOVATION?

- *Consider: The **costs** of open innovation vary widely. If you are investing in early startups, your investment can be preset in the low tens of millions. If you are engaging in small pilots to learn, any given project might land in the low tens of thousands. Costs for an industry consortium or a university sponsorship will depend on the goals. Be sure to compare your costs honestly to the plausible costs of doing nothing—if you're overtaken by a competitor or the industry makes a dramatic shift while you're unprepared, the costs will be enormous.*
- *Consider: You have **other relevant resources**, beyond dollars. Equipment, expertise (including science, engineering, manufacturing, supply chain, sales, and finance), lists (customers and suppliers), and other in-kind resources can be hugely valuable in open innovation.*

Open innovation will take some attention, time, and money. Are you prepared for that?
What resources are truly ready to fire?

Our company spends every single resource on highly efficient operations. No margins. No rainy-day fund. No spare capacity.	If we cannibalized the core business, at least a little, we could put resources into open innovation. Nobody wants to do that, but it's not impossible.	We can find some resources, somehow.	We have funds set aside for this.	We have plenty of resources designated for this priority.
O 1	O 2	O 3	O 4	O 5

QUESTION 8: INNOVATION STRATEGY. IS YOUR INNOVATION PRACTICE GUIDED BY A CAREFULLY CONSIDERED GAME PLAN?

- *Consider: Do you have an innovation **theme or thesis** that guides decision-making? Have you articulated what you intend to explore and where you will not go (for now)?*
- *Consider: Is your innovation strategy **well-designed**? That is—are you clear about what you mean by innovation? Does your governance simultaneously invite exploration and make your learnings visible to the organization? Are your staff trained to communicate their challenges, opportunities, and discoveries effectively, regularly, and to the right recipients?*
- *Consider: Is your innovation strategy **effective**?*

We don't have an innovation strategy. Innovation- related decisions are being taken solely based on trends, politics, and buzzwords.	We don't have a specific innovation strategy. When it comes to innovation, we are taking decisions based on our overall goals and individual responsibilities.	We don't have an innovation strategy per se, but our general strategic practices are well-known across the company, and we rely on those for innovation, as well as for our core business.	We have an innovation strategy but it is not very clear or actionable, therefore it can't guide decisions very well.	We have a very clear and well-defined innovation strategy that we are always using for decision-making purposes.
○ 1	○ 2	○ 3	○ 4	○ 5

Add up your answers to see your final score.

7–14	**15–29**	**30–35**
Your company is facing some serious immediate risks, so this might not be the right time to build full-scale open innovation works. That said, read along! Seek a few silver bullets and low-hanging fruits that can sustain you and help you get ready to dive into open innovation properly once you recover.	This book is perfect for me—we have enough time, resources, and leadership to benefit from open innovation, and we can really use it!	Everything is awesome already—as a master open innovation leader, you can use the book to learn best practices, identify blind spots, study examples from other masters, and deepen your practice.

2
CHAPTER TWO

How Does an Open Innovation Ecosystem Work?

The Ordinary Ecosystem

Let's start by thinking about the ordinary business ecosystem you're involved in, and fully aware of: All business activity unfolds against the backdrop of a complex economic environment in which parties exchange concrete resources including money, products, services, supplies, materials, etc. At a basic level, this ecosystem already exists and your firm is already part of it, exchanging products for dollars with your customers, dollars for supplies with your suppliers, etc. Those dollars continue to move through the market—your suppliers exchange dollars for materials with *their* suppliers, and perhaps ultimately *those* suppliers are your customers. This is the basic business ecosystem that takes place visibly in the marketplace. Here's an oversimplified picture of such an exchange system.

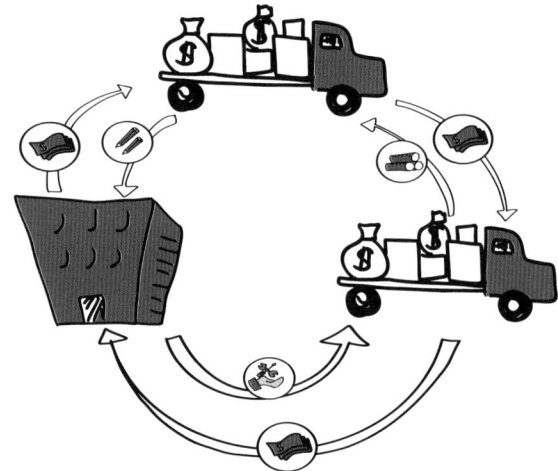

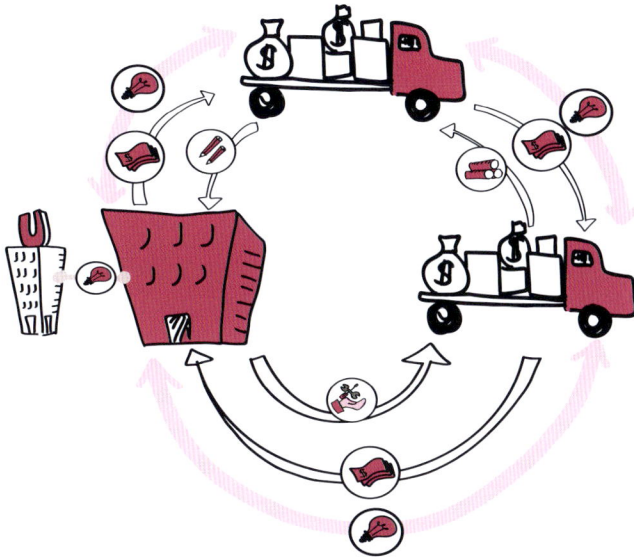

What About an Open Innovation Ecosystem?

There's a second layer of resources that ecosystem entities exchange—ideas, talent, knowledge, predictions, plans, relationships. For example: When your competitor downsizes, you get new access to talent, and you also get a market signal—there's pressure in the system and your competitor has responded.

You might also have relationships with the local university, sponsoring research or visiting their career nights to draw new recruits. You are already participating transactionally in this ecosystem, but you might not be conscious of the ecosystem as a whole, or of the role you play in it. You see things from your own point of view, through your transactional relationships.

All of these entities have more to offer than what they're currently exchanging with you. It's time to bring awareness and intentional contribution to your ecosystem in order to access its full innovation benefits. It's time to leverage the differences

between organizational capacities to enrich the entire ecosystem and weather systemic change. This is the open innovation ecosystem.

Why the Open Innovation Ecosystem Works

Other entities in the ecosystem can do things you can't do, and vice versa. These distinctions are not (merely) a matter of preference or mindset—they are structural. For example, consider incentives: University professors are compensated and honored based on the tenure system, which relies substantially on publication, which in turn relies on the discovery of previously unknown or unproven phenomena. This constraint means that professors will operate on the edges of what's known, and they will tell the world what they're learning. It also means that commercializing their work will be very difficult—the work is too new, and to a professor, keeping a new finding under wraps during the commercialization process will seem like a bad idea relative to sharing it with the academic community. Furthermore, depending on the university, the technology transfer policy might *dis*incentivize commercialization.

On the other hand, corporate employees are compensated based in substantial part on the firm's performance in the open market. They are rewarded through salaries, bonuses, and stock for finding ways to reduce costs and increase profits. They have specific job descriptions and incentive plans that make working in risky or (worse yet) uncertain spaces seem like a bad idea—the structure is designed to keep the core business going.

Startup founders are compensated only to the extent they create a valuable business. They will invest their time and energy in what seems like the best path to value, even if that means tolerating substantial risk. Learning up front about accounting rules, sunshine regulations, or manufacturing practices will seem like a waste of critical resources.

29

Open innovation leverages these differences in how entities can and want to operate. When a corporate sponsors university research, the firm gets access to the very newest ideas, and the university could potentially get access to practical infrastructure—together the pair can envision a path by which new ideas reach people and change lives. When a corporate partners with a startup, the corporate gets access to new solutions early, and to a fast-moving team that is laser-focused on a specific solution. The startup gets access to funding and/or to the mechanisms of scale. Together they can reach far more people than either could alone.

Beyond these one-on-one pairings, more complex relationships drive synergistic possibilities. When the corporate, the university, and the startup world are all connected, ideas have a chance to move from imagination to impact much faster. Moreover, talent has a much faster path to move from the university into a just-right spot in the ecosystem, whether that is a startup or a corporate—that's because people inside of all these organizations know each other well.

A thriving innovation ecosystem brings ongoing awareness of and access to other entities and their activities, opportunities to develop one-on-one as well as more complex partnerships, and a tendency toward stability as interconnected entities with ongoing exchange will tend to pull each other into balance. This last idea, known as homeostasis, deserves additional attention.

Homeostasis

Imagine a simple biological ecosystem that includes just clover and rabbits (our thanks to Linda Booth Sweeney for suggesting the example). This system will tend to remain in balance: If weather conditions create a bountiful year for clover, the rabbit population will increase until it overgrazes clover, at which point the rabbit population will drop for lack of food, making room for clover to grow back.

This is homeostasis, but it's fragile. If one external crisis affects one partner, the system could collapse entirely. More complex ecosystems have more ways to manage stress. In other words, the more complex an ecosystem is, the more its resilience increases.

Add foxes to our ecosystem, for example.

While an increased rabbit population would indeed stress the clover, the additional rabbits also *reduce* stress on foxes by making their nutrition easier to reach. The fox population increases until they cull enough rabbits to relieve stress on the clover. The reduction in the rabbit population increases stress on the foxes, reducing their number in turn. In the background, wastes from the animals provide nutrients for the clover—exchange between all three entities serves to provide additional stability.

A real ecosystem would include dozens or hundreds more entities— such as insects, flowers, trees, microbes, bees and mice. Each player is involved in a lavish number of simple and complex exchanges. Stress is shared across this entire network of exchanges. No single exchange pathway can put the whole ecosystem at risk when it breaks.

A thriving open innovation ecosystem will have this kind of stability as well—startups, corporates, governments, service providers, and other entities all offer different strengths and have different needs and vulnerabilities, mitigated through the exchange network. This stability is a key benefit of ecosystem participation.

What Does a Healthy Open Innovation Ecosystem Look Like?

A healthy open innovation ecosystem includes a rich diversity of entities actively involved in multiple simple and complex exchanges. People tend to know each other across entities, and see each other regularly in planned and unplanned moments.

Often, one or more than one organization arises to intentionally encourage the ecosystem, tracking entities, holding events, and making introductions. In a thriving ecosystem, startups know how to meet someone at a corporate and vice versa; University faculty, students, and staff see a variety of ways to enter the entrepreneurial ecosystem; government entities know where to go to find expertise, etc.

How Can You Benefit from the Open Innovation Ecosystem?

When you make a deliberate ecosystem play, you give yourself access to a wide array of benefits. Engagement with multiple partners allows you to chain opportunities together. For example: Imagine a healthy ecosystem in which institutions maintain ecosystem-friendly policies. In such an ecosystem, a BigCo in the electronics industry might sponsor research in a number of different relevant departments in multiple universities in the geographic region. Under one of those projects, a professor and a postdoc might come up with a novel medical device technology. They report their finding to their corporate sponsor. The sponsor encourages them to commercialize the idea, and introduces them to a venture capital (VC) investor interested in providing the initial funding provided certain steps are followed. The postdoc is happy to step out of academia temporarily to spend time commercializing the device, and the professor is happy to support the project while maintaining their faculty position. Through their extensive experience in the industry, both the professor and the BigCo innovation leader have connections to science, technology, and business experts who can help. The BigCo innovation leader points the postdoc (we'll call them a founder now) to a commercialization leader inside the BigCo who knows how a medical device comes to market and has a relationship with the Food and Drug Administration (FDA). The VC investor introduces the founder to a lawyer who is willing to take the risk of being paid after the funding arrives. The postdoc formally registers as a corporation, and gets good advice from the university about how to sort out healthy equity sharing with

31

the university, the professor, and the VC investor, who in turn sorts out healthy equity sharing of their portion of equity with the BigCo. The BigCo agrees to pay the costs of a proof-of-concept (POC) project that will generate data to support next steps in device commercialization, and the funds arrive just in time for the work to begin. The agreement is carefully constructed with timed exclusivity, that is, the BigCo gets to do the first POC provided the approvals move quickly enough. The founder will explore other partnerships, but pursue them only after the BigCo gets its data. If all goes well, the BigCo and the startup will work together through multiple stages, perhaps a joint research project followed by an in-market pilot. If all of that goes well, the BigCo may acquire the rights to the device, and the postdoc will, as they have always intended, return to the academy as a professor to generate more ideas and more future founders.

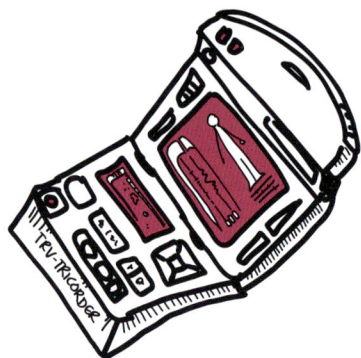

This activity generates a broad array of benefits: The device itself, the related patent(s), data to support research, data to support marketing, answers to questions about customer need in the present and future, stronger relationships among all players, a deeper talent pipeline, a deeper intellectual property (IP) pipeline, and more.

In a thriving ecosystem, synergistic possibilities arise across entities, for example: Key players in the automotive industry formed a coalition with key players in robotics and artificial intelligence

(AI) to move forward on the self-driving car, a challenge requiring all three types of expertise and multiple types of organizations.[1]

Simply through your presence in the room with outside partners, you get a chance to "hear" about ideas and trends early through active participation in the ecosystem—you're right there to hear what other organizations are thinking about, looking for, trying on, and stopping. Your presence also puts you on the radar for new voices and rising talent in your industry, and the adjacent spaces. Over time, you gain recognition as a validated partner with multiple people who can vouch for your company's experience and trustworthiness when needed. Being trusted in the ecosystem increases your magnetism for further partnership, and for talent.

How Can You Contribute to the Ecosystem to Keep It Thriving?

In the above example, healthy practices, inside and outside of each institution, make it easy for information, ideas, and resources to flow. For example:

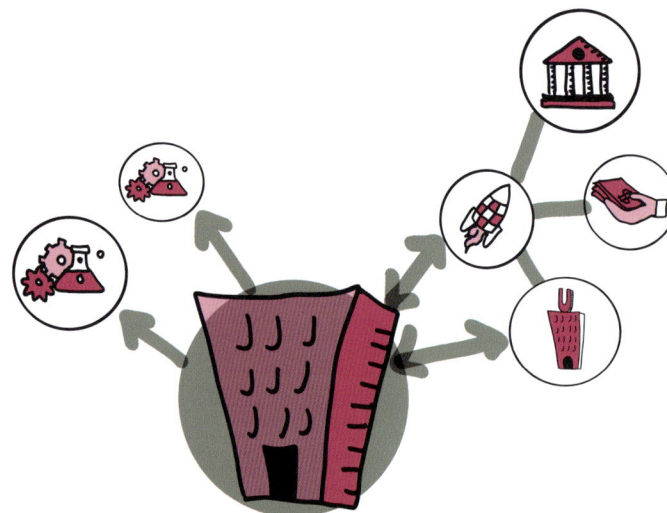

- BigCo staff are engaged in the ecosystem—not just the open innovation leader but also operational staff such as the commercialization expert. They are encouraged to participate in the ecosystem and support startups (or at minimum, they are not discouraged).
- BigCo staff have strong industry and business relationships outside of the building, such as with the investor.
- The BigCo demonstrates its commitment to collaboration by paying for costs. The internal payment process supports speedy delivery of payments.
- The university has entrepreneurship-friendly practices—for example, the Technology Transfer Office limits the amount of equity demanded so that there is plenty of equity left to motivate founders and investors.
- The university understands how commercialization works, helps to teach founders what to do, and connects founders with partners of various kinds.
- Government entities make it easy and quick to certify the corporation, and make it clear and consistent what has to be done to approve the technology's safety.

You can adjust the policies inside of your own organizations to make them as healthy as possible, and you can influence other entities.

The ecosystem is the backdrop for every interaction with any partner—the ecosystem determines how freely capital flows, whether there is enough of the right kind of entrepreneurial, scientific, and engineering talent in your region, and your reputation as a partner, just to name a few important factors in your innovation success as a corporate. So you need to participate. Furthermore, you need to participate as an active contributor, as well as a beneficiary. That two-way flow of energy from each entity, to and from others, is the ecosystem's source of strength.

Showing up (for example, through event sponsorship) is essential but not sufficient. Large firms bring a unique capability stack to the ecosystem:

- Your marketing budget already has funds intended to increase your visibility.
- Your staff has extensive expertise in a number of domains, including technical specialties, regulations, and compliance.
- You have extensive real-world resources (e.g., space, equipment, supplies, bandwidth, etc.).
- Your commercial goals are strong, clear, explicit, and short-term.
- You need outside partners to address your long-term goals.

Open Innovation Is Ecosystem Engagement

Tapping into the ecosystem and deriving ecosystem value for your company begins with building from what you're already doing, and what you already know you need. To begin, just show up. Build relationships by sending staff to attend and participate actively in ecosystem events hosted by investors, universities, other

33

corporates. To extend your ecosystem presence, increase your visibility by sponsoring and hosting events yourself. Sponsor university research, become a limited partner in relevant venture capital firms. General, lightweight ecosystem presence like this offers you a glimpse into which entities are operating in the ecosystem and what opportunities can arise.

The real benefits begin when you partner with other entities to learn by doing and create value together. In *Open Innovation Works*, we detail six different ways you can truly leverage the power of the ecosystem to vault your organization into the future.

Introducing the Engines

In later chapters, we'll go deep into these six open innovation "engines." We'll explain how to select the right one(s) for your firm, how they work, and how you can make them your own. For now, a quick summary of each.

35

Startup Accelerator

Corporate-hosted educational and men-torship program with a fixed term and a cohort. May provide investment funds in exchange for equity. May provide funds with no equity required. Nearly always provides in-kind support such as space, equipment, materials, and/or expertise.

Benefits: Learning (market, technological, scientific), potential long-term return on Investment (ROI).

Startup Incubator

Corporate innovation incubators gener-ally provide subsidized space, support activities, and, ideally, some access to the core business.

Benefits: Low-cost access to information about startups and industry weak-signals.

Corporate Venture Capital

The firm supplies capital to companies with at least mild strategic relevance, in exchange for equity, with direct ROI as an important goal.

Benefits: Visibility, potential ROI.

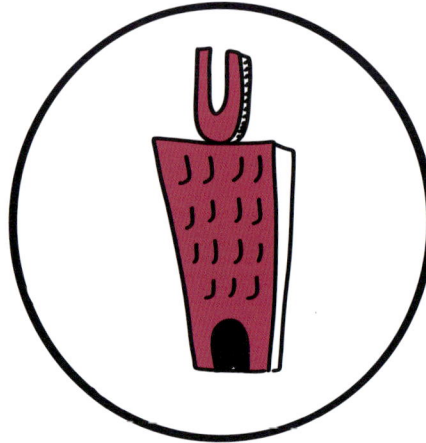

Prove-out Journeys

This is our umbrella term for the practice of working with individual partners, separately, in different ways as appropriate to circumstances, often as a deepening series of collaborative experiments.

Benefits: Risk-limited opportunities for massive learning.

University Partnership

The university's mandate is to explore and investigate. This complements the firm's mandate to commercialize. A common form of partnership is sponsored research.

Benefits: Early awareness of research and technology breakthroughs.

Consortium

A consortium gathers established market players with different expertise and business models to create something that none could create alone.

Benefits: Technological and market leaps.

Now: With these engagement engine concepts in the back of your mind as near-future possibilities, turn your attention to the present. Who is already present in your neighborhood? What are you already exchanging with them? And what benefits might come from deepening your connection across the ecosystem?

Exercise Ecosystem-mapping

As we described above, you are already participating in your ecosystem, for example, as a client to some entities and as a vendor to others. As you expand into open innovation, your work is to get involved in your ecosystem in the places where new insight is being generated. Create a visual map of your ecosystem to inform your journey. Use this map to identify existing relationships that could give you more, and gaps that call for new relationships.

PREPARE

1. Find your backbone organization(s).[2] Chances are, there already exists at least one entity in your area/industry devoted to developing, enhancing, and maintaining the entrepreneurial ecosystem. For example, Boston/Cambridge has the Massachusetts Life Sciences Center,[3] and Southern California has the Alliance for SoCal Innovation.[4] Universities often play a key role.[5] Find out who is doing this work and reach out. If no such backbone exists yet, this is something to start talking about with partners!

2. What's happening in your region/industry already? Identify current activities and start showing up.
   a. Consider meet-ups, competitions, university poster events, etc. Find these in industry publications, mailing lists from the most engaged entities in your ecosystem, Meetup.com., etc. In all likelihood, some of your employees are already participating—find out how!
   b. Show up. Attend in-person and online events. Participate in asynchronous discussions. Become visible. Don't wait to perfect any sort of strategy, just start shaking hands and asking questions. If you can easily help someone out, do it. You can start building your reputation as a good partner even before you know what kinds of partnerships you want.

3. Educate yourself on prior mapping efforts. Leverage any ecosystem mapping the backbone organization(s) or other community members have already done. The life sciences entrepreneurial community in Los Angeles has an attractive example.[6]

SCAN AND MAP

Your goal here is to find insight and opportunity—don't worry about comprehensiveness or perfection, you can leave that to the backbone organization(s).

4. Identify the players in your ecosystem, starting with any existing map. You can do this with physical or virtual sticky notes (as in software like Mirro or Mural).
   a. Start with any existing ecosystem map you can find.
   b. Place yourself at the center of the map.
   c. Add your most accessible partners—those with whom you already have relationships. Include vendors (by category, since you likely have thousands), clients (by category), existing partners, friends.
   d. Add any partners you already know you need, even if you do not yet have a formal relationship. For example, you might know you need startups who are exploring relevant technologies in the market, or you might know you need university partners who are looking at crucial scientific ideas. Consider educational organizations, startup accelerators, investors and government agencies focused on innovation and entrepreneurship (e.g., the small business administration).
   e. What do these entities have that you want? What do they want that you have? For each entry, note their gifts (as labeled arrows pointing from the partner toward you) and needs (as labeled arrows pointing away from you). You can validate these assumptions when you meet.

5. Who is already collaborating?
   a. How are the entities working together? What conversations and partnerships are already in play that you should join?
   b. Look across your own organization. What departments within the organization might already have partnerships going?
   c. Update your map accordingly.

6. What might we do together? Given the map you now see, what possibilities emerge? Where can you go deeper? What gaps are calling to be filled?

You have an idea now of the kinds of entities and relationships that exist in your environment. This should whet your appetite for partnership by revealing entities you should be connected with but aren't yet; relationships you should benefit from that don't yet exist, or exist without your organization.

Open innovation is a way to generate those relationships, deepen them, and generate value from them. You'll need one or more open innovation engines to access that value. And before you create those engines, you'll need to get your internal stakeholders aligned. Hold a vision of your current and desired ecosystem in mind while you work through the Open Innovation Dashboard.

Ecosystem Radar

Icons to indicate type of entity

 Government

 Corporate

 Research (University or research institute)

 Startup

 NGO

 Small Business

 Other (make your own icon)

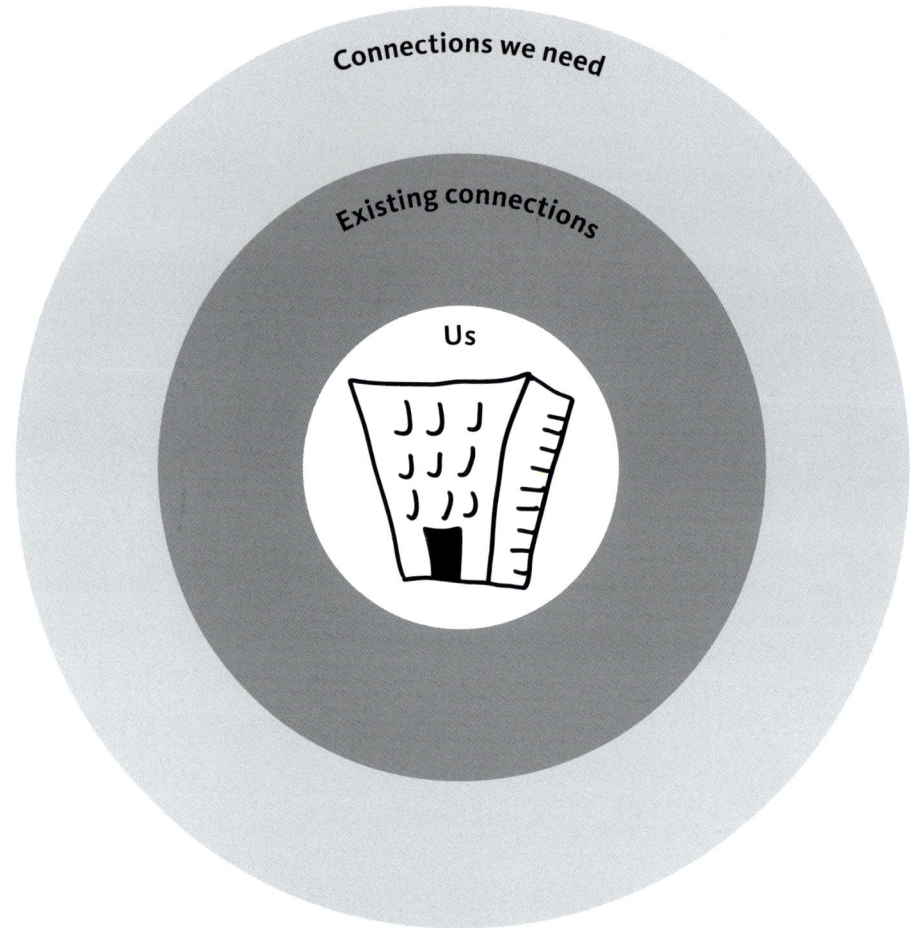

Connections we need

Existing connections

Us

Ecosystem radar - an ecosystem mapping tool
CC by Open Innovation Works

3
CHAPTER THREE

The Open Innovation Works Dashboard

As you can see, open innovation is an intricate affair, not a "one-size-fits-all" or a "shoot-and-forget" endeavor. Earlier, we named six open innovation efforts of different shapes and sizes. Your goals and your resources might drive you to invest in one or more types of engine over others. The decision of which engine to choose needs to be deliberate, congruent with your company's overall ambitions, and—as we have learned the hard way—*made in concert with key stakeholders* whose input weighs heavily on the success or failure of your efforts.

To aid companies in discerning which open innovation engine is right for them, with the proper alignment across all involved stakeholders, we have designed the Open Innovation Works Dashboard.

A bit of history: In the early days of Diana's business, the Corporate Accelerator Forum, Diana embarked on a project that required her to interview dozens of corporate open innovation leaders. One key frustration kept bubbling up: Alignment—agreement between corporate stakeholders about what should happen. Over and over again, she heard about carefully designed open innovation initiatives that died on the vine and promising partnerships that took one step before disappearing. And over and over again, the culprit shooting down these opportunities was stakeholder alignment *inside the large organization*. This observation resonated deeply with Diana's own experience as a corporate open innovation leader, and has been confirmed by research from the Massachusetts Institute of Technology (MIT) and InnoLead as the biggest challenge to startup engagement activity.[1] The challenge was clear—but how to solve it?

"Most corporate open innovators I meet insist that their organization is among the most difficult when it comes to stakeholder alignment."
- Diana Joseph

Diana worked with Dr. Arthur Boni to develop a new innovation dashboard,[2] grounded in a well-known management system called the Balanced Scorecard[3] and in experience with Diana's clients. The new dashboard was designed to generate alignment among internal stakeholders and provide a foundation for measurement.

In the years following the release of the initial version of the dashboard, we have improved our understanding of organizational alignment and open innovation through the work we have done with companies around the world. These sector-diverse, hands-on experiences have led to several improvements to the original template. We've tested our latest iteration with dozens of corporate innovators and are pleased to share it here. This one-page tool is designed to foster dialog between key stakeholders about the purpose of your innovation initiative in strategic terms, the tactical requirements of success, and where you stand as a partner in the ecosystem.

Aligning Stakeholders

The Open Innovation Works Dashboard brings two key benefits. First, as promised, it supports alignment across your company with regard to your open innovation efforts. Second, the tool helps you make a discerning choice around which open innovation engine(s) you need given the entire context of your company. Through a series of straightforward reflection questions, the dashboard helps you establish your position on key considerations that will guide your decision. (We recognize that, in practice, your organization may already have committed to a certain engine before you're able to get started with the dashboard—in that case you'll use the dashboard to guide

yourself and your stakeholders toward the positions they need to hold to make that engine successful.)

Here's how it works: You create alignment by inviting stakeholders to co-own the open innovation plan, process, and outcomes. That happens when they trust that their input is taken seriously, and that core leadership is solid. There's a bit of a tension there—you need the process and key characters to be robust, solid, and trustworthy, and at the same time, flexible and open to input. How can you be solid and flexible at the same time? The answer is to frame your stakeholders' input as helpful to your core intentions, no matter what they say. When they have useful ideas or guidance, add them. When they have contrary ideas,

43

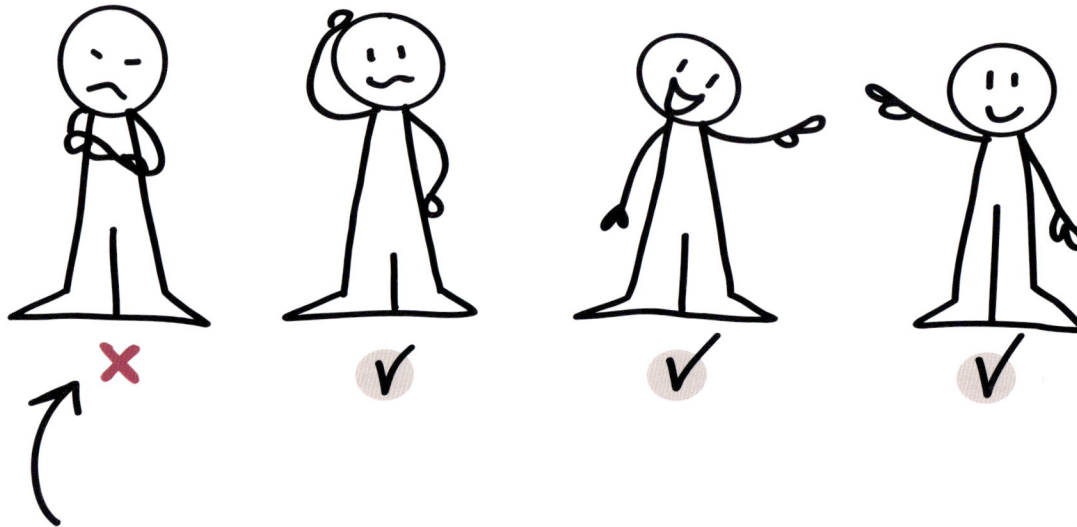

be grateful for the powerful feedback, and figure out how to address their position. The dashboard itself provides a trustable third-party frame: You don't have to persuade them of what the right topics are for discussion, those are displayed in black and white. Depending on your stage, the ideas may be a bit tender, so don't include anyone you think is deeply hostile to the idea and might try to sabotage it.

To complete the dashboard, you'll collaborate with the business stakeholders whose resources, attention, or approval you need in order to move forward. You will collectively address key questions about the business, through a series of interviews, a workshop, or a combination of the two. You will need insights and attention from all relevant stakeholders, even (perhaps especially) those that differ from your own perspective. (You don't need to include anyone who fundamentally hates the whole idea of open innovation. Any potential saboteurs can get used to the

idea later, after implementation.) Depending on the organization and your role in it, you might complete the dashboard yourself and test it with your stakeholders, or you might use an unfilled copy as a basis for cocreation.

Use the dashboard to invite your stakeholders to make their shared positions visible. Once you do this, you'll have a shared language for recognizing success, as well as when you're going off track.

How will you do that in practice? Download the dashboard template or simply use the cover flaps of this book: fold them to form the dashboard. Either way, plan to iterate frequently—we recommend using an erasable whiteboard marker or sticky notes.

Open Innovation Dashboard

Prior Organizational Pledges

Company's Vision and Mission
Your firm's existing published vision & mission statements

Company's Innovation Strategy
Your company's innovation theme or thesis

Open Innovation Intentions

What we want to achieve
What is your strategic intent for open innovation and how will you measure the outcomes? (Financial, customer and sustainable development)

Open Innovation Maturity
What are you ready to take on?
E.g., We've never done any collaboration before; we have some examples but they didn't work; we want to try new things; we are already experts

Appetite for Risk
What is your company willing to put at stake for the benefits of open innovation
E.g., financial risk, brand risk, customer relationships and nothing

Tactical Changes Our Firm Needs To Make

Cultural Change
What changes are we willing to make to our culture so that open innovation can work?

Structural Change
What steps will we take to formally encourage open innovation?
E.g., incentives such as bonuses, public recognition, promotions, "upside"; management structures such as job descriptions, reporting hierarchy and oversight practices

Processes
What processes we will create or change for our open innovation works?
E.g., simplified contracts, fast-tracked payments and procurement

Resources Committed
What resources will we commit toward our open innovation works?
E.g., funds, staff time, brand, equipment, materials, customer access and suppliers.

How our company will learn
What will we do to ensure that our open innovation insights are recognized and delivered to the stakeholders who can benefit from them? E.g., inclusion of stakeholders in projects, reports, meetings, events and direct access to your board.

How our company will adapt and integrate discoveries based on what we learn
How will we accommodate the changes needed to take advantage of what we're learning?
E.g., changes to product lines, new business models and new supply chains.

The Open innovation Dashboard CC by OpenInnovation.works

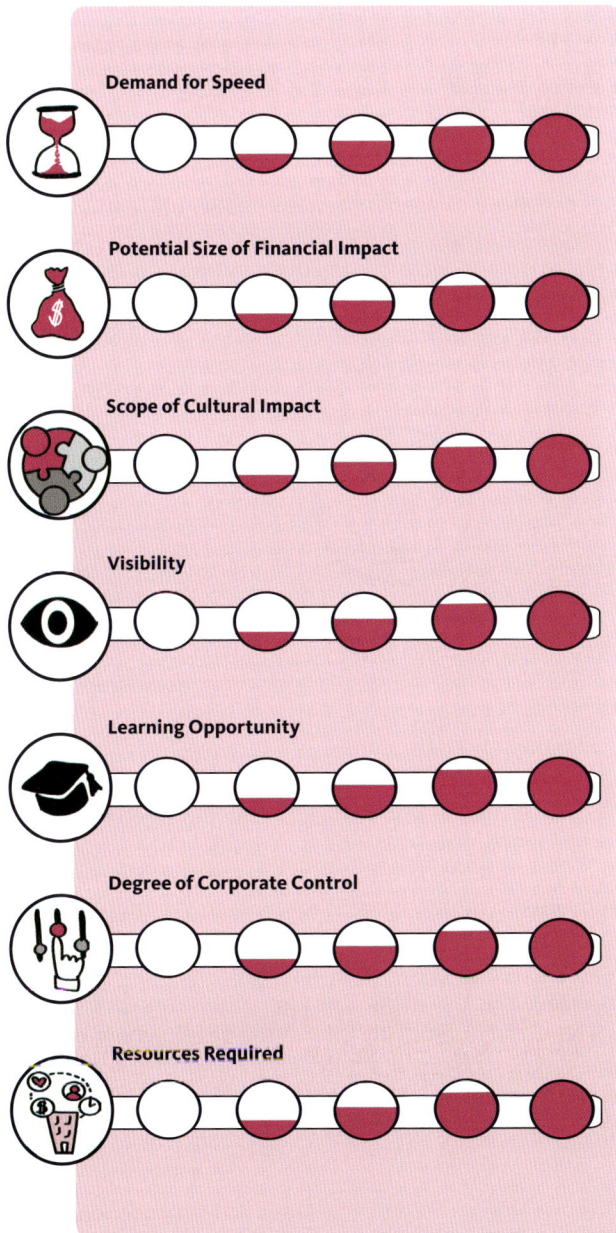

Demand for Speed

Potential Size of Financial Impact

Scope of Cultural Impact

Visibility

Learning Opportunity

Degree of Corporate Control

Resources Required

Looking at the Dashboard

Begin on the left side of the dashboard by addressing fundamental matters where misalignment tends to trip companies up in their open innovation efforts. Use this section to come to explicit recognition of, and agreement on, your firm's central commitments, strategic intentions, current readiness, and tactical positioning. You'll return to this map regularly over time to demonstrate your continual adherence to the agreement, and to remind your stakeholders what they agreed to for their part.

The second section of the dashboard, on the right-hand side, invites you to identify your specific intentions and capacities concerning your future open innovation practice. You will assign numerical values ranging from 1 to 5 to each aspect of your willingness and ability to engage in open innovation. Use the insights gathered on the left side to guide your scoring of the factors on the right. In the upcoming pages of the book, you'll compare these scores to the matching capacities each open innovation engine can deliver. This will allow you to discern which engine(s) are right for your organization.

Enough said. Let's put the dashboard under the microscope for a better look at its elements.

47

Download the
Dashboard
here.

Prior Organizational Pledges

Company's Vision and Mission
Your firm's existing published vision & mission statements

Company's Innovation Strategy
Your company's innovation theme or thesis

Open Innovation Intentions

What we want to achieve
What is your strategic intent & how will you measure the outcomes? (financial, customer and sustainable development)

Open Innovation Maturity
Who are you ready to take on? E.g., We've never done any collaboration before; we have some examples but they didn't work; we want to try new things; we are already experts

Appetite for Risk
What is your company willing to put at stake for the benefits of open innovation E.g., financial risk, brand risk, customer relationships and nothing.

Tactical Changes Our Firm Needs To Make

Cultural Change
What changes are we willing to make to our culture so that open innovation can work?

Structural Change
What steps will we take to formally encourage open innovation? E.g., incentives such as bonuses, public recognition, promotions, "upskill" management structures such as job descriptions, reporting hierarchy and oversight practices.

Processes
What processes we will create or change for our open innovation work? E.g., simplified contracts, fast tracked payments and procurement

Resources Committed
What resources will we commit toward our open innovation work? E.g., funds, staff time, brand, equipment, materials, customer access and suppliers.

How our company will learn
What will we do to ensure that our open innovation insights are foreground and delivered to the stakeholders who can benefit from them? E.g., inclusion of stakeholders in projects, reports, meetings, events and direct access to your board.

How our company will adapt and integrate discoveries based on what we learn
How will we accommodate the changes needed to take advantage of what we're learning? E.g., changes to product lines, new business models and new supply chains.

Fundamentals for Alignment

On the left side of the dashboard, propose, test, and discuss what's underlying your open innovation intentions, and what changes you'll undertake.

Prior Organizational Pledges

Alignment can be tricky. Innovators are often perceived as agents of chaos hostile to tradition. You can reduce friction for your open innovation work by pledging public allegiance to those aspects of your firm's past and present that serve, or at least do not detract from, open innovation. Your very first task in asking stakeholders to align is to demonstrate your own alignment with your organization's existing positions—show and declare that your intentions as an innovator or innovation team are to enhance key elements of what the organization is already doing.

VISION AND MISSION

Open innovation needs to contribute to your organization's overall ambition and place in the market and society, so start by writing down your organization's vision and mission statements. If your company hasn't established these statements, use whatever language your organization uses to let customers, shareholders, and other interested parties know what your broad intentions are.

Filling in this initial box serves as a persistent reminder of the contributions open innovation should make to your organization's overall objectives. Use the published commitments your company already has in place to confirm for all stakeholders that you're on the same team.

Some good news about alignment here: Vision and mission statements are typically crafted to be noncontroversial, so agreeing to them should be easy for you.

COMPANY'S INNOVATION STRATEGY

A well-defined innovation strategy is powerful for companies as it provides a clear roadmap for growth and adaptability while ensuring alignment with the company's core business strategy. A strategic approach to innovation ensures efficient resource allocation, boosts market presence, and enhances overall organizational resilience, making it vital for success and relevance in today's dynamic business landscape. If your organization already has an innovation strategy, name the key strategic intent here.

If your firm does not yet have an articulated innovation strategy, you can leave this box blank. The open innovation practice you are creating may eventually inform the development of an overall innovation strategy, but don't let the lack of one slow you down now. (When you're ready to build your innovation strategy, check out our prior book, *The Corporate Startup*[4]).

Open Innovation Intentions

If you're reading this book as a first step on your journey to open innovation, you'll be starting from scratch in this section. If you're tuning your open innovation practice, you'll have some thoughts to get you started. Either way, this section is where you'll name your specific goals for open innovation, and reflect on your organization's readiness and risk tolerance, in preparation for decision-making.

WHAT WE WANT TO ACHIEVE

Outlining the organization's specific purpose for investing in open innovation is crucial. You'll want to consider, at minimum, your financial goals, your customer goals, goals for organizational culture, and goals for social and environmental impact. Challenge your stakeholders to name the fundamental purpose of the upcoming open innovation practice—or invite them to challenge the purpose you have identified. Will you name here the general **themes** your company wants to pursue with open innovation? Or will you be a bit more specific, naming types of ideas you want to pursue (we call this more specific approach a **thesis**). Use this section to open a sincere dialog about the true intentions behind your organization's open innovation investment. This topic might deserve its own book one day. In the meantime, be ambitious, strive for alignment over perfection, expect to adjust as you learn.

OPEN INNOVATION MATURITY

Depending on your company's open innovation maturity level, certain open innovation engines might be better suited than others. It's vital for all stakeholders to recognize your company's open innovation experience or lack thereof.

This dashboard section will spark a dialog about the company's familiarity with open innovation. Is this a first-time endeavor, or has the company already learned some lessons from open innovation previously? Understanding the company's history with open innovation is key to making informed decisions about the upcoming open innovation play. Hint: You thought about this when you completed the quiz, back in the first chapter. Look back at the quiz for a reminder!

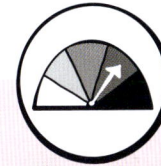

APPETITE FOR RISK

One of the most captivating topics in the dashboard is the company's risk tolerance. The dashboard creates an opportunity for all stakeholders to articulate how far out of the organizational comfort zone they are prepared to go in order to make sense of an uncertain future.

Depending on the outcome of this discussion, some open innovation engines might be eliminated from consideration due to risk, including perceived jeopardy to assets that the company's board may not approve. At the same time, the discussion is an opportunity to expose opportunities where extra risk can bring extra reward. Alignment on the topic of risk is crucial.

49

Tactical Changes Our Firm Needs to Make

So far in the dashboard, we have looked at your firm's historical positions, desires, and appetites. From now on, we are going to look at the things the company is willing to change for open innovation to succeed. The company might have more or less flexibility on different items. Naming your plans in the dashboard puts all stakeholders on the same page, and also constrains and guides which open innovation engine you should select.

CULTURAL CHANGE

By culture, we mean the values, beliefs, and behaviors that characterize your staff's interactions with each other and the outside world. Are you willing to change the culture of your firm in order to accommodate open innovation effectively? For example, will you encourage and demonstrate faster (and less deliberative) decision-making in low-stakes circumstances? Will you reward experimentation? If you have declared cultural change goals earlier in the dashboard, you will certainly need to be willing to change the culture. Either way, your organization's willingness to shift your culture should significantly inform your choice of open innovation engines.

STRUCTURAL CHANGE

What structures is the company willing and/or capable of setting up or changing for the open innovation initiative? Where will the open innovation engine report in your hierarchy? How will open innovation participation be incentivized? Are you willing to disincentivize the status quo? The matter of structural change is closely related to cultural change.

This section of the dashboard forces a conversation about what kinds of structural changes are acceptable in order to get the open innovation outcomes you want, and which structural elements are sacred and must be tolerated.

50

PROCESSES

Processes are surprisingly important in the success of an open innovation endeavor—not to mention other endeavors! Appropriate processes reduce friction to smooth the path for partnerships. Conversely, incorrect processes (either excessively rigid or overly flexible) can jeopardize the investments.

Therefore, it is essential to engage in a discussion about the processes the company is willing to establish or modify for the open innovation initiative before kicking it off. For example, today your procurement process might be designed for established large vendors, and begin with three months of contract negotiation, followed by a six-month onboarding process. Are you willing to create a pocket process to pay open innovation partners in a more timely fashion? Your choice can help to determine who your partners should be, and therefore which open innovation engines are suitable.

RESOURCES

The specific resources that the company is prepared to invest in its open innovation endeavor will significantly influence the choice of an appropriate open innovation engine.

For instance, if the company is unwilling to provide investment dollars, it will be immediately evident that a corporate venture capital (CVC) play is not viable. You'll prefer arrangements in which material, expertise, and equipment are sufficiently meaningful to your counterparts, perhaps an incubator or partnership journey.

In your alignment work, be sure to discuss exactly where resources will come from. Who will spend time? Which budget will be reduced to make space for open innovation?

As you decide what resources to invest, keep in mind the costs you'll incur if you do nothing and thereby miss an important technological, business, environmental, or cultural shift. The cost of doing nothing is potentially enormous. What are you willing to spend to prevent that loss?

51

Adaptation Plans

The one guarantee open innovation can offer is a learning opportunity. Too often, however, firms waste this opportunity for lack of a net to catch the learnings when they arrive. To properly grasp that opportunity, build practical pathways for lessons learned to reach relevant staff, and to impact your business decisions going forward.

HOW OUR COMPANY WILL LEARN (CHANGE BASED ON INSIGHTS)

This section of the template is devoted to ensuring that the insights gained from its investment in open innovation permeate across various departments and become seamlessly integrated into the company's overall operations. Name specific approaches for knowledge transfer and implementation across the organization. In short, how will key personnel hear about what the open innovation engine learns?

HOW OUR COMPANY WILL ADAPT (CHANGE TO ADAPT NEW TECHNOLOGIES, SERVICES, AND BUSINESS MODELS)

Learnings need to be reflected in actual business choices on the ground. How will your organization take on the practical discoveries of your open innovation work? Who will lead and participate in converting discoveries to new or adapted product/service lines or sales/marketing practices? What actions will they take to enact these changes? What resources can they draw on in the process?

The Scales

On the right side of your dashboard (and the back cover flap) are seven scales indicating seven distinguishing facets of different open innovation engines. For each of these, choose the numerical value that represents what you are looking for in an open innovation engine, guided by the discussions you've captured on the left side of the dashboard. Perhaps you're looking for a high financial impact, but you're not in a rush and you don't need much, if any, cultural change. Or perhaps you're looking for a big learning opportunity, and you'll accept a more modest financial impact for now. Keep balance in mind—if you expect a high financial impact, quickly, with no resource infusion from your organization, you're describing a pipe dream rather than an open innovation engine. Later in this book, we'll show you how each innovation engine maps to these scales. Note your scores in the template or on the back cover - we recommend you use erasable markings because you're likely to want to iterate as you learn about the options.

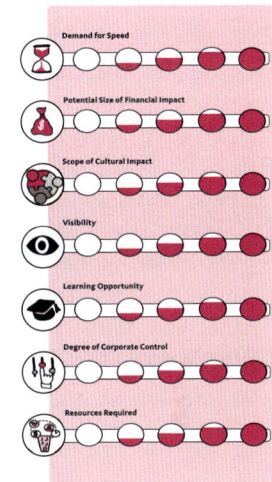

DEMAND FOR SPEED

How long do you have before your stakeholders require financial impact on the firm's bottom line?
(In most cases you can provide learning impact almost immediately.)

How to decide: What is your firm's patience level? Time after time, we see open innovation efforts shot down after failing to meet unreasonable demands for production of return on investment (ROI). We're not in the quick-fix business here, we're looking for discoveries in unexplored spaces. Will your organization wait an appropriate number of years for your industry before demanding a financial return? Or do you need to show ROI right away? Your patience or impatience will constrain which engines you can use. Take influence from the open innovation intentions you named on the Fundamentals side of the dashboard—your intentions will help to determine the appropriate patience level for your firm.

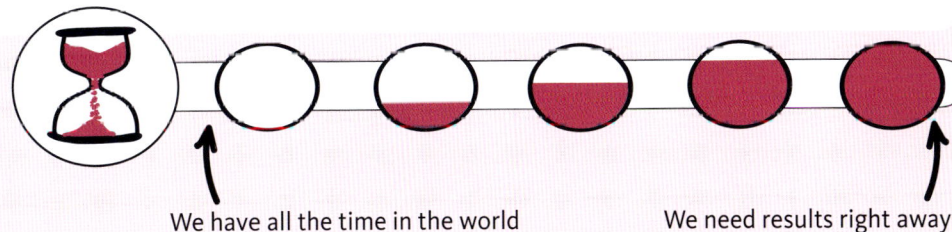

We have all the time in the world   We need results right away

POTENTIAL SIZE OF FINANCIAL IMPACT

How much money do you need to make from this engine? Is this mainly exploratory, or is it expected to (eventually) deliver cash at a level that's relevant for your business? Some engines are more likely to result in profit than others.

How to decide: Your chief financial officer (CFO)'s perspective is a crucial consideration. An effective CFO understands what the firm needs financially in order to move forward, and at the same time, they understand the perspective of board members and shareholders with regard to innovation and the company's boundaries. Realistically, do you need high ROI to justify the project, or do you need to emphasize other goals such as learning? Do you want financial scrutiny, or do you want to avoid it? Like your Demand for Speed, the size of financial impact you need will be influenced by the open innovation intentions you declared on the left side of the dashboard.

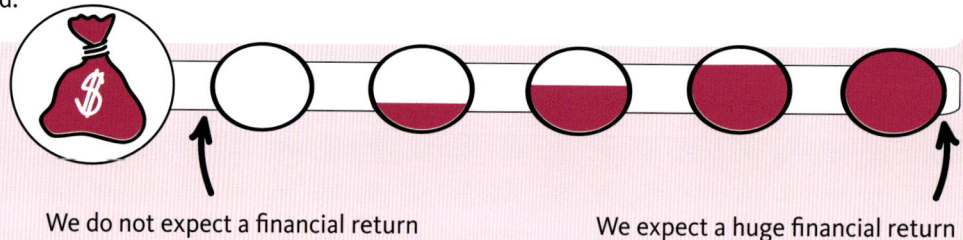

We do not expect a financial return   We expect a huge financial return

VISIBILITY

Are you looking for this effort to help your firm become famous for its innovation? At the other extreme, are you looking to keep your learning and experimentation as private as possible? Some engines are more public than others.

How to decide: In some conditions, the budget and mandate to move forward with open innovation is directly tied to visibility goals. If the open innovation effort reports to the marketing department, obviously your direct purpose is to be seen. On the other hand, if your purpose is mainly to expand your products, services, and business models, it's absolutely fine to keep your efforts quiet. Visibility strongly depends on your intentions, especially your appetite for risk.

Even if you land on the quiet side, it's important to stay in alignment with business requirements. Your CFO and/or compliance team can guide you on minimum reporting requirements for open innovation efforts in your region, industry, and organization.

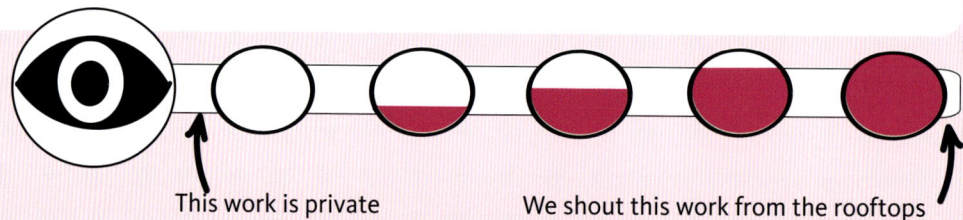

This work is private   We shout this work from the rooftops

SCOPE OF CULTURAL IMPACT

On the left side of the dashboard, you explored how much cultural change you're willing to make in order to facilitate open innovation. On the right side, identify the reverse: to what extent do you require your open innovation efforts to *drive* culture change across your organization? Some engines are designed to invite corporate staff to learn new mindsets, practices, and rituals. Others take place rather far outside of the core business and don't impact corporate staff at all.

How to decide: Your open innovation effort might be born out of a cultural change intention, for example, to make your staff more innovative—this was certainly one of the goals at the Citrix Startup Accelerator Seed Fund when Diana worked there. In this case, your desire for cultural impact puts your score high on this scale. If you're mainly after ROI, or happy to attach new businesses without integrating them, or if your culture is already where you want it to be, your position here could be low.

55

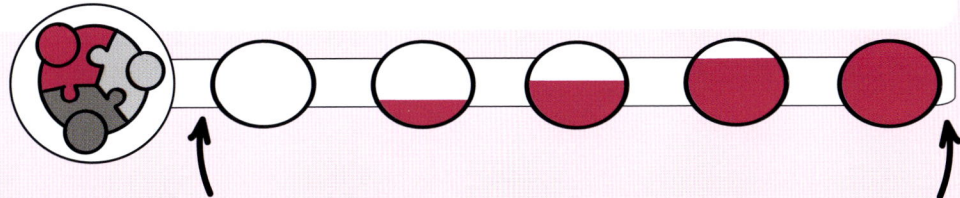

We don't expect this work to impact our culture   We rely on this work to change our culture fundamentally

DEGREE OF CORPORATE CONTROL

To what extent does your organization need to control your partners? If you will need to place significant constraints on their day-to-day choices, that position will help to determine the set of engines you can consider. Conversely, if you don't plan to provide any guidance at all, that will also narrow the set of engines for you to consider.

How to decide: Every act of open innovation entails a certain relinquishing of control—after all, the other parties are your partners, not your employees. Ask yourself: If a partner does something you don't like, what will that mean? If it means disaster, your position on the Control scale is high. If it means you get to learn something, you have room to choose a lower level of control. Keep in mind: Divergence is a crucial source of creativity, innovation, and learning. How much divergence are you willing to welcome into your open innovation engine? Your position on this scale needs to align appropriately with your maturity, your risk appetite, and the culture/process changes you're planning, per the Fundamentals side of the dashboard.

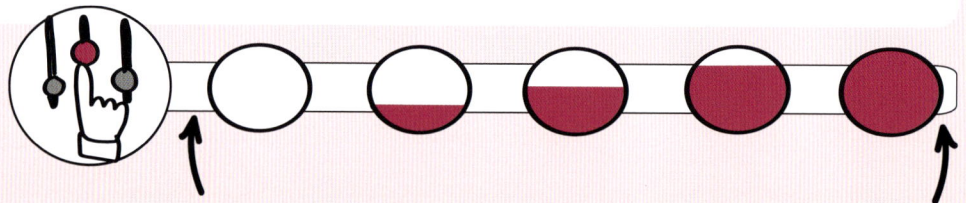

This work will be fully independent of control from the core business   This work will be fully under the control of the core business

LEARNING

How much learning do you expect to gain from this experience? If your main goals are visibility and financial ROI, learning may be a smaller factor. On the other hand, consider this: Learning is the one outcome that can be guaranteed from any open innovation exercise—you'll start learning on Day One. The amount you intend to learn (read: change) will help to determine which engine(s) you'll invest your time into.

How to decide: Hopefully, you're not tempted to choose the "not at all" location on this scale—what a waste that would be! Of course, you're going to learn something, the question is how much. The more you lean into learning, the higher the risk that you won't make money. That's because you will learn the most in the most uncertain spaces. To complicate the matter, if you're going to be high visibility, you may get more financial pressure, and more pressure to avoid mistakes. So, your Financial Impact, Visibility, and Learning scales are in a system together. It's worth thinking through what you want that system to look like. How the Fundamentals play in: Your appetite for risk will constrain how much you can learn, and your commitment to a learning practice will determine how far that learning can go. If you're not really planning to receive technological, market, or other lessons learned into the main business, there's no point in leaning into the learning goal.

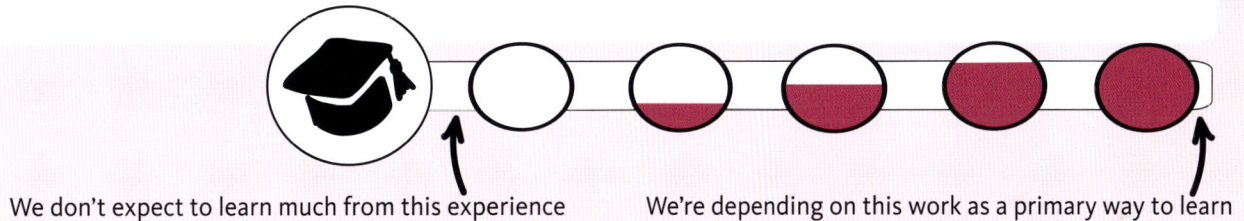

We don't expect to learn much from this experience ← → We're depending on this work as a primary way to learn

57

RESOURCES COMMITTED

You've already discussed this, and you know whose time and treasure you'll bring to bear. Now make it explicit: How much time and treasure will you invest in this effort?

How to decide: Easy peasy—use this scale to visualize the understanding you developed in the Resources Committed box to the left on the Fundamentals side of the dashboard.

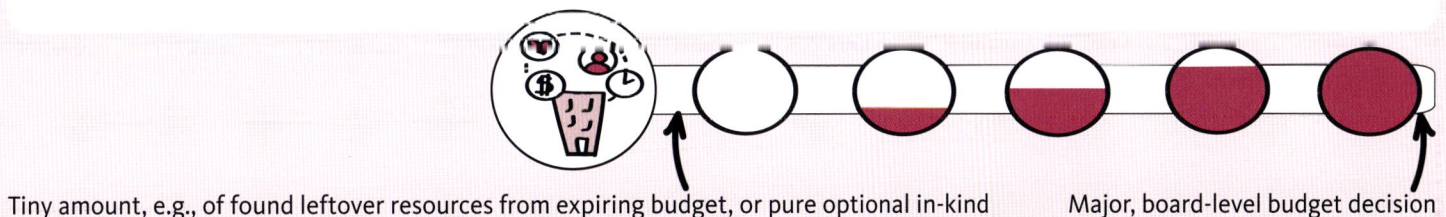

Tiny amount, e.g., of found leftover resources from expiring budget, or pure optional in-kind ← → Major, board-level budget decision

Exercise Stakeholder Alignment

Adapt the following process to your particular organization, your particular stage of open innovation (Are you starting from scratch or updating the path that's already unfolding?), and your role in the organization (Are you a senior leader yourself? Someone who's already responsible for open innovation? A frontline staffer with a good idea?):

1. Identify key stakeholders—those who will contribute to and/or benefit from open innovation efforts. Include:
   - Decision-makers who can say go or no-go on open innovation at large, or on any particular initiative specifically. This might include one or two executives or members of the Board with the mindset to champion these efforts in the face of challenge.
   - Staff whose time and energy will be needed (e.g., to evaluate or learn from partners, develop new processes or agreements).
   - Managers whose staff will be spending time and energy on open innovation.
   - Any additional enthusiasts who do not fall into the above categories.
   - *No need to include people who will gain nothing from open innovation, or who, for any reason, are likely to hate the idea.*

2. Using the template available or the cover flaps of the book, prefill your dashboard with reasonable guesses, using pencil, sticky notes, erasable marker on a whiteboard, or other changeable media. Do not get attached to your guesses, intend for them to change. We recommend starting with the Fundamentals side (on the left), and iterating multiple times until you're satisfied that the two sides make sense together.

3. Get your senior stakeholders on board with the process in whatever way suits your organization, perhaps through brief one-on-one meetings. Use the dashboard to learn their positions and preview yours. Be sure they are literally or figuratively holding the pencil, sticky notes, or erasable marker as you communicate. Listen. Ensure clarity on what they are willing to invest, change, and give up, as well as what they want. Change your master dashboard in response to their thoughts *while maintaining responsibility for the logic and coherence of the final outcome.* You are the owner of the concept—be a solid, listening leader.

4. For more stakeholders with more designated time and interest, hold an interactive meeting/workshop with up to ten people to review the vetted dashboard, section by section—discuss and finalize.

5. Once you're done, it's time to lock in commitment on the changes. Anyone contributing resources, including time, will need to sign off or be informed through their managers.

6. Prepare your leaders for a resource request! If you've done cocreation right, they'll be expecting it.

7. Get ready to revise—as your plans meet reality you'll discover insights that need to alter your dashboard.

8. Build an open innovation advisory board from your most invested dashboard stakeholders. Plan to update and keep them apprised on a regular basis. With their partnership, plan to change what you're doing as you learn.

Download the Dashboard here.

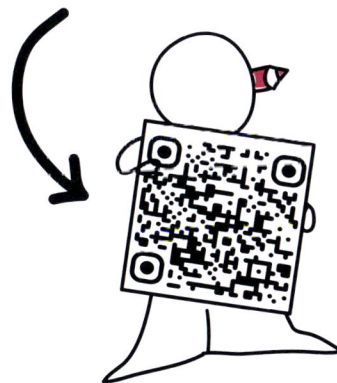

Open Innovation Dashboard

Prior Organizational Pledges

Company's Vision and Mission
Your firm's existing published vision & mission statements

Company's Innovation Strategy
Your company's innovation theme or thesis

Open Innovation Intentions

What we want to achieve
What is your strategic intent for open innovation and how will you measure the outcomes? (Financial, customer and sustainable development)

Open Innovation Maturity
What are you ready to take on?
E.g., We've never done any collaboration before; we have some examples but they didn't work; we want to try new things; we are already experts

Appetite for Risk
What is your company willing to put at stake for the benefits of open innovation
E.g., financial risk, brand risk, customer relationships and nothing

Tactical Changes Our Firm Needs To Make

Cultural Change
What changes are we willing to make to our culture so that open innovation can work?

Structural Change
What steps will we take to formally encourage open innovation?
E.g., incentives such as bonuses, public recognition, promotions, "upside"; management structures such as job descriptions, reporting hierarchy and oversight practices

Processes
What processes we will create or change for our open innovation works?
E.g., simplified contracts, fast-tracked payments and procurement

Resources Committed
What resources will we commit toward our open innovation works?
E.g., funds, staff time, brand, equipment, materials, customer access and suppliers.

How our company will learn
What will we do to ensure that our open innovation insights are recognized and delivered to the stakeholders who can benefit from them?
E.g., inclusion of stakeholders in projects, reports, meetings, events and direct access to your board.

How our company will adapt and integrate discoveries based on what we learn
How will we accommodate the changes needed to take advantage of what we're learning?
E.g., changes to product lines, new business models and new supply chains.

Demand for Speed

Potential Size of Financial Impact

Scope of Cultural Impact

Visibility

Learning Opportunity

Degree of Corporate Control

Resources Required

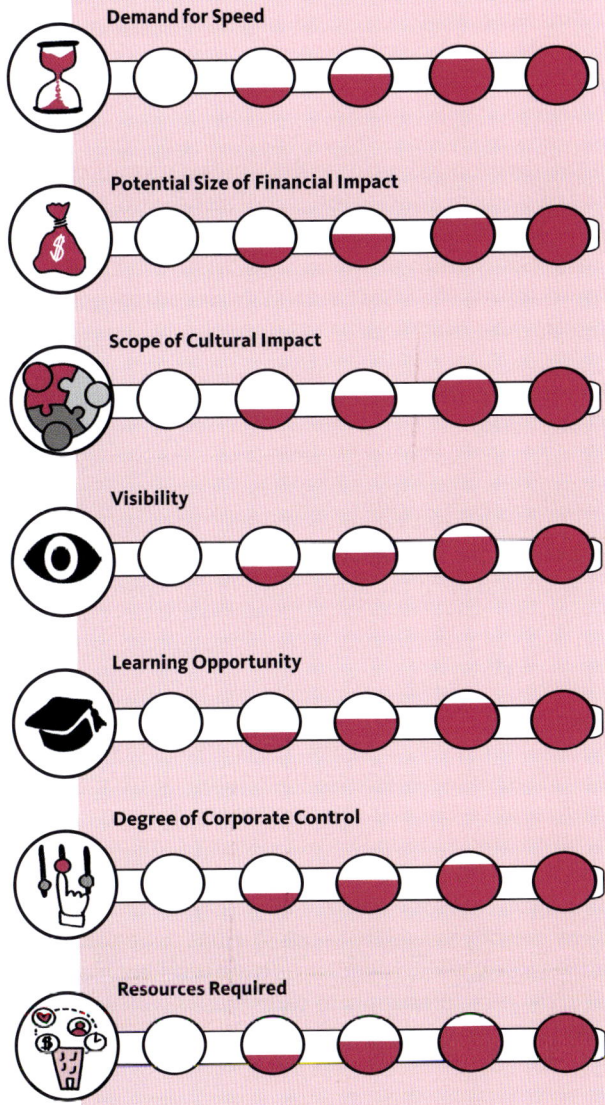

Your Open Innovation Squad:
Who Do You Need and What Are Their Responsibilities?

- Executive champion:
  - Holds a wide aperture as they view the ecosystem, ensuring the organization is scanning for weak signs.
  - Communicates vision and expectations inside the company.
  - Resource approval.
  - Sends cultural signals (e.g., honoring the discovery of dead ends, as well as celebrating wins).
- Open innovation team:
  - Manages open innovation processes.
  - Ensures the flow of desired cultural influence between the organization and its partners.
  - Ongoing ecosystem engagement.
  - Slays dragons—addresses the inevitable obstacles that arise.
- Frontline staff (e.g., engineers or scientists directly engaged in partnerships):
  - Direct partnership responsibilities.
  - Learn and communicate what is learned.
  - Manage boundaries (i.e., know which intellectual property belongs to whom, what can and cannot be promised).
- Managers of frontline staff adding additional open innovation responsibilities:
  - Carve out time for staff, engage backup support where needed.
  - Celebrate learnings, even from the discovery of dead ends (sometimes known as failure).

At least one person from each of these ranks should continue to weigh in as you move forward. Consider this your
Open Innovation Advisory Board.

61

4
CHAPTER FOUR

Optimizing Your Open Innovation Practice

Through the dashboard, you've developed a solid shared statement of your organization's positions, and secured stakeholder buy-in for the journey. Soon, it will be time to select the open innovation approach, or the strategic mix of approaches, that best suit(s) your company's unique needs, and dive in.

First, some key principles that will apply no matter which engine(s) you choose.

Be Partner-Friendly

Before we dive into the engines, we want to highlight one crucial factor that applies to all of these engines and any open innovation partnership: Being "partner-friendly." This is especially crucial in partnering with startups. In these elephant-and-mouse relationships, as the elephant, you need to be careful not to step on your mouse. That's easy to do and hard to recover from. And it's not just for the mouse's sake. We've argued that in an environment of dynamic change open innovation is necessary for long-term corporate health. You need to know: The mice all know each other. Startup founders will ask your prior partners what it was like to work with you. If you develop a reputation for squishing mice, that's the end of your ability to partner with them, and the end of your ability to use startups to help you reach into the future. While friendliness is most salient in startup partnerships, the principles apply to partnerships with anyone.

There are really just three commandments: Thou Shalt Communicate, Waste Not Thy Partner's Time, and Bring Only Joy with Thy Brand:

Thou Shalt Communicate:
- Be findable. Make it easy for potential partners to find the person or process that can bring a partnership forward.
- Be responsive. Tell partners your time frame for response, and stick to it. Reach out if you run into delays. Say no when you mean no. Say yes *only* when you mean yes. Provide feedback, even to candidates you're not going to partner with.

Waste Not Thy Partner's Time:
- Pay for time and materials, especially if your partner is a small organization. Often, you'll need a look at what the partner can do before you can commit to anything significant. If your partner needs to spend significant time preparing specialized materials or versions of something just for you, compensate them. It's great for your reputation and costs an amount of money that matters for them and is a rounding error on a rounding error for you (likely in the hundreds or very low thousands of dollars). You can put this on a company credit card—no procurement process required.
- Know what processes your partner will face in working with you. This is an important one because corporate innovation teams turn over frequently. A brand-new innovation leader might not know what you don't know about partnerships, for example, how long the vendor process takes, whose signatures are required. Onboarding a new vendor can take months, even up to a year—and a project or entire startup can die for lack of funds in that time. So, it's imperative that the innovation team knows what to tell their external partners, in advance. Better yet, develop a fast-track process for partners and get them paid on time.

Bring Only Joy with Thy Brand:
- Be aware and intentional about the impact of your brand on your partners' ability to function with investors and in the market, especially if you'll own some equity—that's a public behavior that all other partners will see. Consider carefully: Is it good for your partner(s) to have a strong association with your brand? Will it open doors for them or provide credibility? If so, speak freely about your partnership, give your partner permission to do the same and provide access to your brand assets as they do. On the other hand: Could a strong association with your brand cause problems for your partner? For example, if you take a large equity stake in a startup, could that chill attention from competitors who might also invest? Or from general investors who think you're there to acquire the startup at a discount?
- Wield exclusivity carefully. It's OK to ask a promising partner to focus on you—but with limits. Keep your exclusivity demands in check so your partner can continue to grow. Limits to consider: Time (make it temporary), regional (for a limited time, ask to be the only partner in your region—city, state, or country, for example), industry (for a limited time, ask to be the only partner in your industry). Right of First Refusal (ROFR or RFR) is a type of exclusivity and deserves similar consideration.

Communicate

Communicate regularly, clearly, and transparently to all stakeholders as a crucial foundation for trust. Everything you communicate must be accurate as you understand the truth in the moment. It is, of course, sometimes necessary to keep information bounded—you still come across as a transparent communicator when you're firm, clear, and consistent about the boundaries—what you will and won't share. Tune your broad communications to the right frequency, answer questions as best you're able in a timely fashion.

Measure in Phases

We explained in our earlier book, *Innovation Accounting*, that value creation happens through a process—that's why traditional accounting won't work for innovation, open or otherwise. Each stage of the process has different goals. If you measure *exploration* work with *outcome* measures, you're almost guaranteed to make value-destroying decisions. Think back to the Borders story at the start of *Open Innovation Works*: Borders used *efficiency* measures (good for measuring outcomes) to evaluate *exploratory* activity (the uncertain space of newborn e-commerce), and therefore chose (with great confidence!) to outsource crucial activity to a (future) competitor, a suicidal move.

Tie your measures to appropriate goals for the particular stage of your work. For each engine, we'll offer you metrics tied to three phases: Preparation, operation, and outcomes. The specific ways you measure each of these phases will differ according to the engine.

Keep Your Stakeholders Engaged

You've worked hard to develop a team of involved and interested internal stakeholders across multiple managerial levels. Keep them involved. Invite them to visit your open innovation engine(s). Invite them to support partner efforts directly. Ask them to help you slay dragons (address emergent challenges). Elevate them as speakers and mentors. Share findings at their preferred cadence. Ask them to guide integration of results into the business. Consider formalizing a small group of stakeholders as an Open Innovation Advisory Board with regular meetings. Above all, keep listening, and respecting and using what you hear. If you stop listening, these advocates may turn away or even shut you down.

Plan Your Learning

Our definition of learning is pragmatic: Learning is recognizing a new insight and using it to make a change. In order to receive this benefit, regardless of which engine you choose, you'll need to prepare for it properly.

In your dashboard, you have already zeroed in on what you intend to achieve, e.g., for customers, for finances and for sustainability. You've also zeroed in on commitments of attention and time from internal stakeholders. The work of the innovation engine(s) you choose will place specific internal stakeholders in specific positions of partner interaction. Those stakeholders will be responsible for recognizing discoveries emerging from and with your partners, sharing that learning appropriately inside your organization, and making changes based on what you're learning. You'll want to highlight your learning wins back to your stakeholders/Open Innovation Advisory Board on a regular (minimum quarterly) basis. Think in terms of two main steps: catching insights, and making changes.

Catching insights: Ideally, your stakeholders are spending time directly with your partners, and have an opportunity to be surprised and stretched. Alternatively (or simultaneously), you can build a practice whereby the open innovation engine leadership gathers insights and reports on them to an internal group on a regular cadence. Either way, document insights—they are a primary product of your engine. Certain insights are easily transformed into change by the stakeholder who catches them in the first place. That's fairly readily done. Others require different players and significant investment of time and attention. For each engine, we'll guide you on how to capture insights and use them to drive change.

Making changes: Count a range of types of changes as learning. A tiny change, or a change that takes a great deal of time to come true, still counts as learning. A charming observation with no intention for change doesn't count as learning. Begin by documenting this qualitatively, through stories. This story-gathering process may reveal patterns that you can document quantitatively.

Mix and Match

Combining open innovation engines can be very powerful—if you mark high scores on the financial impact and learning scales, you can engage in corporate venture capital (CVC) as well as university collaboration, and address these motives separately. University sponsorships can build relationships that lead to prove-out journeys. Incubators can produce startups that are well-suited to acceleration. Mix and match carefully to ensure healthy signals—if some accelerator teams get CVC funding, make sure that doesn't mean there was something wrong with the other teams (or be transparent up front about the competition).

Diving into the Engines

Your journey toward open innovation excellence begins with the decision-making phase and extends to the meticulous planning and execution required to integrate the chosen engine(s) seamlessly into your company's operations. This holistic approach ensures that open innovation becomes not just an isolated activity but a transformative force deeply embedded in the core of your company's strategic initiatives.

Selecting the right open innovation engine represents a significant step toward actualizing open innovation within your company. Develop a clear understanding of the engines that align best with your context and discern those that do not—this way, you shift from imitating competitors to purposefully defining your company's approach to open innovation. In this deliberate step you craft an approach tailored to your company's unique attributes and requirements.

This strategic move ensures that your investment in open innovation is aligned with your company's specific needs, and at the same time secures the necessary support from top management. It's imperative to recognize that for open innovation to truly yield value and garner executive backing, it must be intricately woven into the fabric of your company, and reflective of its distinct nuances.

Let's take a look at six different approaches to open innovation—from here we'll call these the engines. Each engine guide in this section clarifies the specific capabilities of that engine, and lays out how to set up, run, and learn from them, and, when the time is right, to sunset the effort.

65

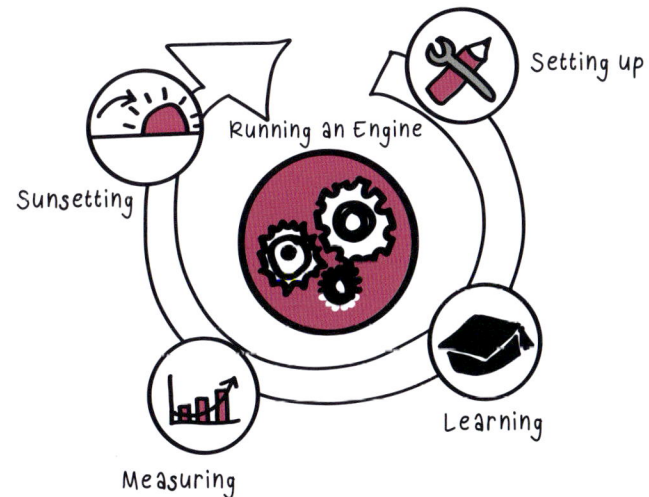

Running an Engine

Setting up

Sunsetting

Learning

Measuring

Which one(s) will you choose? For each engine, consider its distinct features and trade-offs, and match with the specific requirements and context of your company. From that basis, you'll be ready to make an informed choice, ensuring that your selected approach is truly fit for your situation and purpose. Keep in mind: Chances are you won't find a *perfect* fit, real life isn't a textbook. Instead, look for a decent fit and then decide—will you change something about your own positions to make a better match (for example, increase or reduce your visibility needs)? Will you customize your engine to be a better fit for your firm (for example, increase cultural impact by creating more opportunities for core staff engagement)?

Open innovation is iterative—as you explore, you'll refine your intentions, expand your organization's capacity, and catch insights to exploit. Bring your discoveries back to your dashboard—revise on a regular basis and shift what you're doing appropriately.

Now for the fun part!

Earlier, you took a good look at your present ecosystem and noted the kinds of relationships and entities you might want to engage. In the dashboard, you and your stakeholders have jointly stated what you intend to accomplish, what changes you're willing to make, and where you stand with regard to key positions.

Now it's time to take action: Choose the right set of open innovation engines for you, and make them come alive.

We've constructed this book so that the positions you take in the dashboard will determine what you will read next. In other words, the next part is a Choose your Own Adventure!

At the start of each engine guide in this section, we've provided a set of capability scales that are an exact match to the ones you've filled out on the template or the back cover flap. The capability scale pages are marked in pink on the outer edge so you can find them easily. Wrap the flap around like a bookmark to compare your positions to the capacities of each engine, side by side. If you're deeply interested in all the engines, read linearly, and test your match with each one as you go. If you want to read deeply only those engines that match your positions, wrap the flap around to each of the six pink-edged pages, one at a time, and decide which engines matter most. Read those guides and feel free to skip the rest.

Speed to Results

Potential Size of Financial Impact

Scope of Cultural Impact

Visibility

Learning Opportunity

Degree of Corporate Control

Resources Required

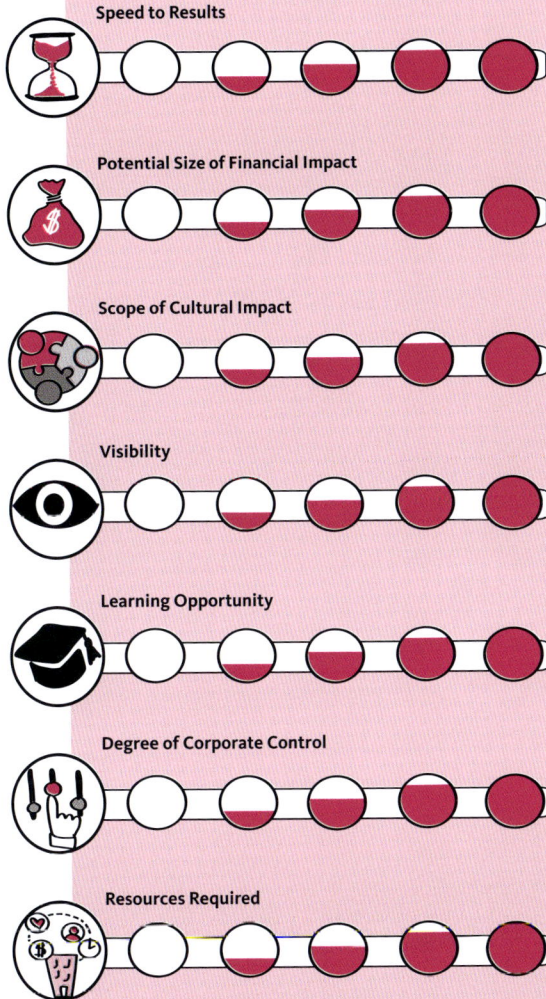

An interest in startups will take you to the Accelerator, Incubator and Corporate Venture Capital (CVC) engines. An interest in universities will naturally take you to the University Partnership engine. An interest in peers will take you to the Consortium engine. The Prove-out Journey engine can be good for any partner type, though we use startups in our examples.

If your ecosystem map (or any other motive) made you hungry to partner with a certain type of entity but your scales are a terrible mismatch, we suggest you read those sections anyway. If an engine interests you enough after understanding what's involved, maybe you can influence your organization to shift positions on the scales and make your desired partnerships more feasible.

Ready?
On to the engines!

67

PART 2

The Engines

5
CHAPTER FIVE

Startup Accelerator

Startup Accelerators. You've heard of them. Large organizations often start their open innovation journey here, perhaps because the startup accelerator model is well defined. Startup accelerators are defined by three basic traditions[1]:

*   selected startups participate in an educational program as a cohort
*   the experience is time-limited, typically ending with a culminating event called a demo day
*   there is some sort of exchange between the organizations, typically cash and in-kind support from the large firm in return for a standard portion of equity in the startups.

This model, inspired by Y-Combinator—arguably the inaugural and certainly the most renowned general accelerator—has set the standard for the industry. That said, each individual accelerator brings its own take on these "rules."

Operationally, a startup accelerator must attract viable startups by persuading founders that the resources on offer are a good match for any equity or other consideration requested, and that the education on offer is just what the startups need. Then the accelerator must deliver on those promises: Providing funds, space, supplies, and equipment, as well as support, programming, and mentorship.

A startup accelerator driven by a large organization such as a corporation has some special advantages relative to third-party accelerators (like Y Combinator). A large organization is an active frontline participant in its industry, and therefore by definition has on board the full capacities needed to participate in that industry. Those capacities, such as physical workspace, equipment, supplies, access to branding, customers, and specialist expertise are invaluable to founders. The nonmonetary resources extended by corporate-based startup accelerators can prove to be as, if not more, valuable than the capital investment. In an accelerator, startups foster innovation and collaboration within a time-bound framework, while generating insights and equity for the sponsoring organization.

Consider how Startup Accelerators stack up on the dashboard scales.

71

Speed to Results

Potential Size of Financial Impact

Scope of Cultural Impact

Visibility

Learning Opportunity

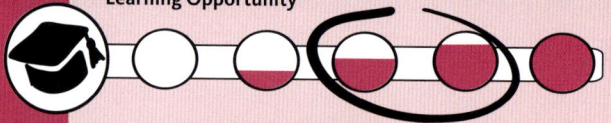

Degree of Corporate Control

Resources Required

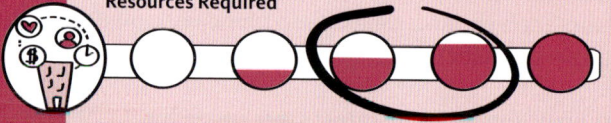

Demand for Speed

Potential Size of Financial Impact

Scope of Cultural Impact

Visibility

Learning Opportunity

Degree of Corporate Control

Resources Required

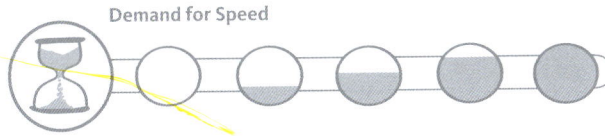

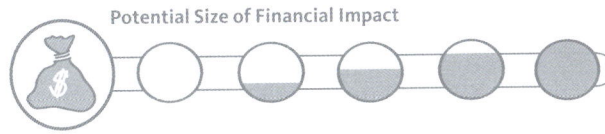

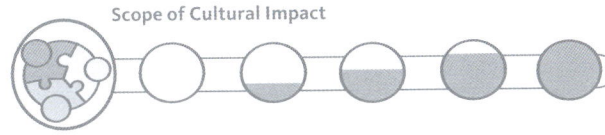

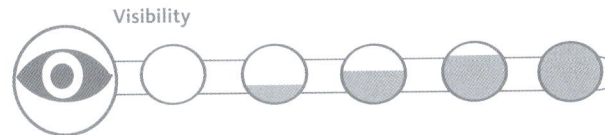

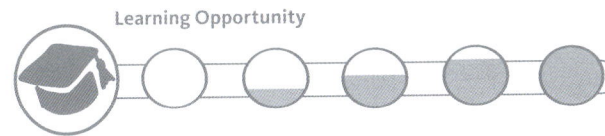

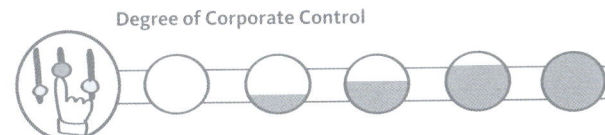

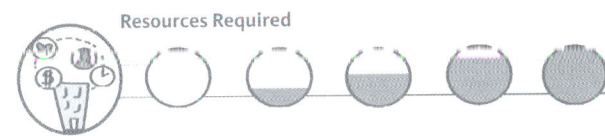

Bend the
back cover flap
over this page
to see your scales
and the Engine's scales
side by side.

Accelerator Scales

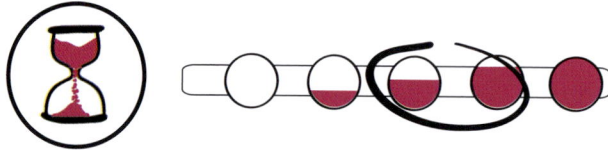

SPEED TO RESULTS:
Learning comes right away, investment is going to take a while.

Accelerators can bring financial income to a large organization in two ways: First, lessons learned from partnership with the startups may be applied in the core business. For example, by working with startups who are your customers (cf. Illumina Accelerator), you learn what your customers need to do to serve *their* customers. This allows you to alter your product or marketing to better serve the entire value chain and make more money through sales. On this path, Speed to Results is as rapid as your sales cycle—simply feed insights directly into your existing sales machine. Second, income can arrive through investment in the participating companies. This can take anywhere from three to ten years, depending on the industry. Does that sound like a long time? Here's why it makes sense: Startup accelerators work with early stage companies. That's because only early stage companies are willing to exchange significant amounts of equity for relatively small amounts of cash/in-kind resources. Once startups are profitable, or even bringing in consistent revenue, the cost of equity will be much higher, and founders' hunger for industry education will be much lower. Partnering with later stage startups can be really powerful, as we'll discuss in other engines, but an accelerator isn't the right model for a startup that's already making significant revenue in-market. Accelerators serve early stage startups—they're not selling a product yet, in fact they might not even have a working prototype yet. They need time and your help, and that's exactly why they want to be in the accelerator. You'll need to have a bit of patience so that they can grow up into profitable or otherwise valuable companies that can generate a financial return on your investment.

If you marked "Demand for Speed" as a 3 or a 4, the Startup Accelerator might be a good match for your needs.

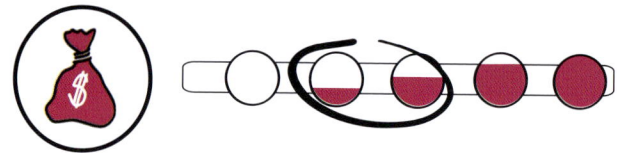

POTENTIAL SIZE OF FINANCIAL IMPACT:
The money is hard to predict.

Because accelerator startups are early stage, the direct impact an accelerator will have on your company's top line is difficult to calculate. There's a chance you'll get lucky and one of your startups will be a big win with a big financial payoff, but you can't count on this. What you can count on: You will generate new insights. Some of those insights could impact the trajectory of your organization, for huge financial impact.

If you are under pressure to generate a substantial, measurable, short-term dollar figure from open innovation, a startup accelerator might not be the right engine for you. But if your financial targets are on the softer side—you marked 2 or 3 on your Size of Impact scale—an accelerator could be just perfect.

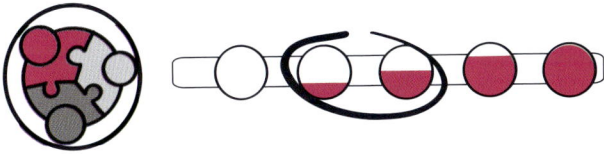

SCOPE OF CULTURAL IMPACT:
Deep, not broad.

Cultural impact is an important reason why large organizations want to engage with startups—they see startup founders as inspiring figures who can show their employees what initiative looks like. That's a fair assessment—engaging with startups really can offer valuable inspiration and an opportunity to glean new approaches to work and collaboration. Cultural impact isn't guaranteed though. Your accelerator will need to be carefully designed in order to generate the impact you're looking for, and you'll need to be realistic about how far that impact can go.

The source of cultural impact from an accelerator is direct contact: Startups join an accelerator per se primarily for the learning opportunity. (At least they should—some might join purely for the cash, and not show up to the learning opportunity. You'll want to screen for that as best you can, especially if you're seeking cultural impact.) That learning comes primarily from the large firm's staff, potentially to include scientific, technical, marketing, sales, regulatory/compliance, and legal. That close contact can be a source of mindset impact for those employees who participate. With a high-impact, culture-focused design, specific employees can be deeply inspired by their experiences supporting startups in an accelerator. However, there will be limits on how many large-organization employees can have this experience and receive this external exposure.

If your goals for cultural impact are important but modest, a startup accelerator can be a viable open innovation engine for you.

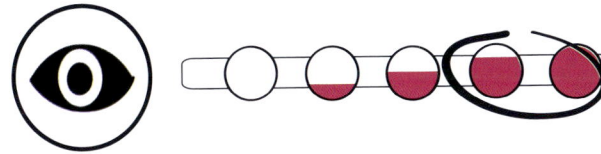

VISIBILITY:
Your accelerator needs to be famous.

Corporate accelerators are generally conducted with a high level of visibility, strategically publicized by the company to attract startups and simultaneously broadcast its commitment to innovation on a broader scale. The intentional promotion of the accelerator opportunity serves a dual purpose. First, it acts as a beacon to draw in innovative startups by showcasing the benefits and resources the corporate accelerator can provide. This external visibility allows the company to tap into a diverse pool of entrepreneurial talent, fostering potential collaborations and partnerships.

Second, the publicizing of the accelerator initiative serves as a marketing strategy, revealing the corporation's dedication to embracing innovation and staying at the forefront of industry trends. By making their innovation intentions known to the world, companies not only signal their openness to change but also position themselves as active contributors to the evolving landscape of their respective industries. This external messaging can positively impact the corporate brand, attracting attention from investors, customers, and other key stakeholders who value and support a commitment to ongoing innovation.

If your company is hungry for visibility, opting to invest in an accelerator program as an open innovation engine might be the way forward for you.

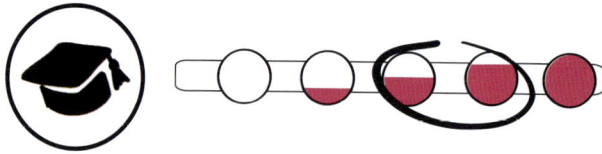

LEARNING OPPORTUNITY:
Organic learning opportunities.

Abundant learning opportunities arise when a corporate accelerator is thoughtfully designed to actively receive and leverage insights. This involves key personnel from the company engaging with the startups so they can clearly understand the technologies, ways of working, and, above all, the reactions the startup's clients have to the offering. This activity can inform conclusions about market trends and technology adoption, conclusions that can (and should) drive decisions in the core operations of the corporation. This is the other side of the coin of cultural impact—when you offer your employees and your founders time to work productively together, you get cultural impact, and you get technological and market learning.

If your company is serious about learning firsthand about new trends and technologies, investing in a startup accelerator program might be the way forward.

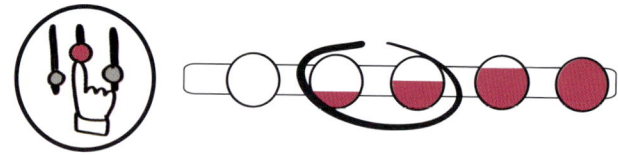

DEGREE OF CORPORATE CONTROL:
Guidance, not prescription.

We've seen highly prescriptive accelerators, but we've never seen them succeed very well. In our experience, successful corporate accelerators distinguish themselves by adopting a guidance-oriented approach. Instead of imposing a rigid curriculum, these accelerators provide startups with a spectrum of valuable offerings, including physical workspace, necessary materials, access to clients, access to infrastructure, and expert advice. This more flexible and supportive model empowers startups to navigate their unique challenges and developmental needs, fostering an environment where innovation can flourish organically. Not coincidentally, this model also causes founders to call on employees of the large firm for their expertise, thereby exposing employees to startup culture, new technologies, and business insights. By prioritizing guidance over prescription, these accelerators allow startups to chart their own course while benefiting from the resources and mentorship provided by the corporate entity, ultimately contributing to a more dynamic and mutually beneficial ecosystem.

If you're willing to provide some guidance by which startups choose work that provides you with insight, a startup accelerator might be a good choice for you.

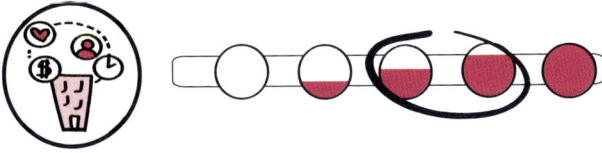

RESOURCES REQUIRED:
You'll feel it, but it's not outrageous.

The accelerator model requires some up-front costs for space, investment, and personnel. These costs can be kept fairly low by using existing underutilized assets and by partnering (for example, if the investment comes from outside investors seeking dealflow). If the firm itself is providing cash in exchange for equity, the financial cost may be higher.

Ultimately, costs depend on the trade-offs you choose. For example, the cost to hire a third party, such as TechStars, may seem high at the start, relative to housing the accelerator internally. Relying on third-party experience may be worth the cost. However, the learning available from a third-party accelerator is much lower than the learning available from an in-house accelerator.

A startup accelerator can be run with a small staff—at minimum a business leader, a technical leader, and administrative support. In-kind offerings may be drawn from excess capacity to minimize cost (for example, the firm may have an unused building floor, good materials with older branding not suitable for sale, equipment with spare run-time, etc.).

If the company is willing to invest in order to access cultural, learning, and visibility opportunities, as well as potentially win financially as accelerator companies grow, an accelerator might be a good fit.

Why Should You Choose this Engine?

Corporate-based startup accelerators provide an intimate view of startups as they explore uncertainty, something that is very difficult to do in a large firm. At the Citrix Startup Accelerator, we referred to this glimpse of the uncertain future as "seeing around corners." This intimate view comes from tight alignment: The firm often provides space, therefore your staff knows right where the founders are in order to observe them; the firm provides equipment, materials, supplies, and expertise, therefore your staff are present when discoveries are made; the firm provides brand power, therefore the startup is motivated to enhance the firm's brand. If the firm takes equity, they are part-owners in the startup, and both sides recognize the shared goal of effective commercialization.

For corporations, the primary benefit of a startup accelerator is **learning**: By embedding with the startups, the firm gets to participate directly in lessons learned about technology or science, the particular industry, business model experiments, and/or the startups' customers' behaviors, demographics, and purchasing patterns. These insights can be invaluable to the organization's strategy. A secondary benefit may be financial. If financial return on investment (ROI) is your primary goal, you will need to limit your admissions to startups that have already figured something out. In other words, you don't get to enter the intimate partnership until most of the key learning has already happened. The more importance you place on short-term ROI, the more limits you place on learning.

That said, ROI from an accelerator is entirely possible over the long term, assuming you're investing and taking equity. Your selection policy will focus on identifying highly qualified teams with real devotion to the project, and your equity stake will keep you tied to the project until ROI arrives in the form of exploiting insights right away, and/or an exit. (Your exit will arrive sooner and small if the next investor buys you out, later and potentially significant if the firm goes public via an initial public offering (IPO) or is acquired for a high ticket price).

Why Shouldn't You Choose this Engine?

As appealing as accelerators are, they're not appropriate for every large firm. Accelerators are highly visible. Any investment payout is likely to be small, or arrive slowly. Finally, corporate accelerators rely heavily on the firm's brand value and interaction with the small company's brand—if that public brand engagement is not desirable, then the accelerator is the wrong engine for you.

Don't choose an accelerator when your open innovation efforts need to produce short-term revenue. If you are engaging in open innovation because your core business is dying, you need immediate revenue. An accelerator will not do this for you, you need a merger with, or an acquisition of, a mature company.

Don't choose an accelerator when you want privacy. A corporate accelerator puts you visibly on the radar for startups and their potential investors, and for your own shareholders and stakeholders. Is that the right move for you?

Finally, don't choose an accelerator if you can't identify startups whose brand would benefit by association with yours. As with all open innovation engines, it is imperative that you benefit the startups. Damaging them will ruin your reputation, not only as a partner but also as an ecosystem participant. If your acquisition targets, your customers, or your beneficiaries would suffer by bringing your brand on board, the accelerator is not the right engine for you.

Making a Startup Accelerator Work

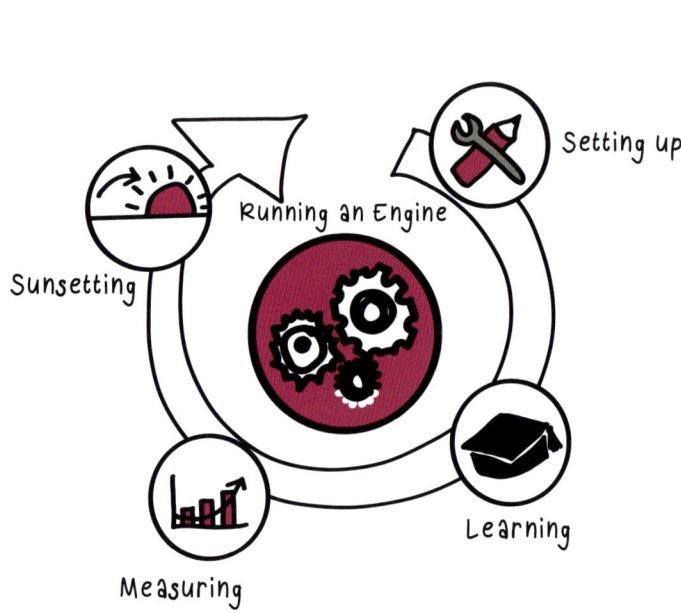

You've decided that a startup accelerator is the best open innovation vehicle for your context. That means you plan to provide resources to cohorts of well-suited startups as a way to learn from their developmental journeys over a limited period of time. You might also want to invest in in them financially, hoping for a return.

Now it's time to decide exactly what resources you will provide, to which startups, over what period of time, and what you'll ask for in exchange.

Setting Up Your Accelerator
Before you engage with startups on behalf of your accelerator, you'll need to let your ecosystem know what you're doing, and create a place into which to welcome the teams you select. There are several areas in which you'll need to prepare: The physical space and equipment, determining what startups will do with their time, and the exchange of value. (You'll also need a marketing plan of course. In this arena we won't say much, we're confident your existing marketing team will know what to do.)

The other setup steps all depend on how value will be exchanged, so let's start there.

DECIDE WHAT BENEFITS YOU WILL PROVIDE
A crucial early decision: You are about to enter into a type of partnership with a group of startups. You're seeking a learning opportunity and a chance for a financial win. What will you offer in return?

In exchange for the benefits you want, you'll provide some benefits to startups. Of course, they value cash—especially the early stage startups that are a good fit for an accelerator. Beyond cash, corporate-based accelerators have some special benefits they can provide that are not available to third-party accelerators such as Y Combinator. Because your firm is already a significant actor in the industry, you are sure to have access to assets of great interest to your startups. These might include technical advisors, customers, equipment, materials,

supplies, and industry- and region-relevant, nontechnical expertise (e.g., HR regulations and user research). The beauty of these in-kind (nonfinancial) assets is that the value to your startups is enormous, while the cost to you is trivial. You might very well have spare equipment time or machines and excess supplies that can be provided at little to no cost. If the accelerator is sufficiently relevant to your staff, you might find that some technical and nontechnical experts from within your organization would like to spend time with your startups over and above their regular work.

Most corporate startup accelerators offer cash and take equity via something like a SAFE note (an industry accepted low-friction agreement template) or a convertible note (an agreement which starts with cash but triggers equity under success conditions later in the journey). But there are many exceptions. REI's Embark engine for new founders provides a small amount of cash and does not demand equity. Google for Startups offers equity-free, non-cash support. Illumina Accelerator strictly required equity in exchange for tremendously valuable equipment, supplies, and investment network access.

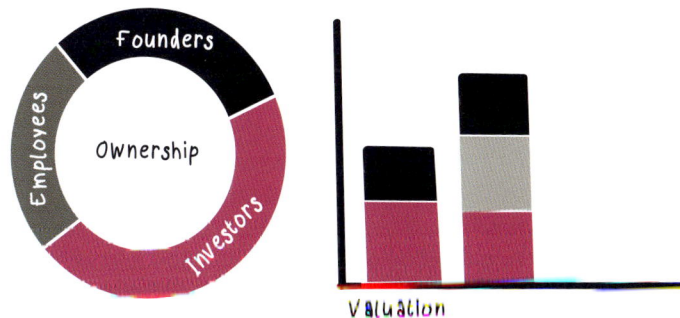

Valuation

Cash is the clearest, simplest way to attract startups. However, it comes with trade-offs. On the internal side, depending on the investment size and number of startups supported, you may invoke more attention than you want from your own chief financial officer (CFO). Externally, you may attract founders experiencing cash desperation, rather than confident founders.

If you are providing cash, consider carefully which budget(s) makes the contribution—the owners of that budget get to set at least some of the metrics by which the project is measured. If the budget comes from marketing, you'll be tracking marketing metrics. If it comes from the product department, you'll be measuring impact on new products. If it comes from external partners, you'll be beholden to their goals. Any stakeholder who provides cash is automatically a partner in the accelerator endeavor: They've decided to give up a crucial resource for you, demonstrating that goals are fully aligned. The tight alignment between your goals and theirs can become a huge benefit, a huge distraction, or even both.

The amount of cash you'll offer ideally lands in a "Goldilocks zone"—not too much, not too little, but just right. If you offer too much cash, you might draw more attention than you want from your CFO. Worse, you might drive the startup's valuation up, making future investment or exit more difficult for them. Further, your presence on the capitalization (cap) table (investment record) as a major investor creates expectations in the market that could damage the startup's other investment opportunities. The ecosystem might think that you intend to acquire, chilling the interest of your competitors in investing, and creating significant risk if you don't ultimately acquire. On the other hand, if you invest too little, your startups might lose ground while they work with you, or decline to work with you in favor of more cash-rich opportunities. Provide enough to make a difference and attract founders, but not so much that you draw extra scrutiny or confuse the market.

If you're not offering cash, you'll need to ensure that the non-cash benefits you offer are sufficiently high to attract highly effective founders. Use assets native to your firm to save your founders money in terms of costs for specialized space such as labs or cleanrooms, manufacturing capability, servers, or supplies. Link your founders to massively valuable experts and insights they couldn't otherwise access—for example, scientific, regulatory, HR, finance, marketing, and sales. Introduce your founders to vendors and customers. Highlight your start-ups on your platforms. If true, show founders that your internal stakeholders are serious about future potential partnership, purchasing, or licensing. Identify and communicate this value to your founders as you recruit. Ideally, the non-cash benefits you offer are unique to your firm—they differentiate you from other opportunities startups could take and attract startups who are already well-matched partners.

Whether your benefits are cash, in-kind, or a combination, should you take equity? This is a common but serious move with consequential positive and negative implications—on the positive side, in addition to the obvious benefit of potential ROI, your co-ownership ensures that your interests and those of a growth-oriented founder are aligned. The incentives are in place for you to work hard together toward growth. Both organizations might also benefit from the mutual brand association. For example, for a genomics startup, having Illumina (a genomics equipment company) as an investor creates a positive signal to other investors, and highlights Illumina's innovative spirit.

On the negative side, the brand association could reduce the startup's ability to raise investment dollars or exit by implying that you'd limit participation from your competitors. You could also reduce the startup's ability to benefit from an exit because they've overvalued the company or given up too much equity. And, of course, you could lose your investment! Chances are nine out of ten investments will fail to pay off financially. If you are taking equity, literal ROI will certainly be one of your key performance indicators (KPIs), and that means you'll need to

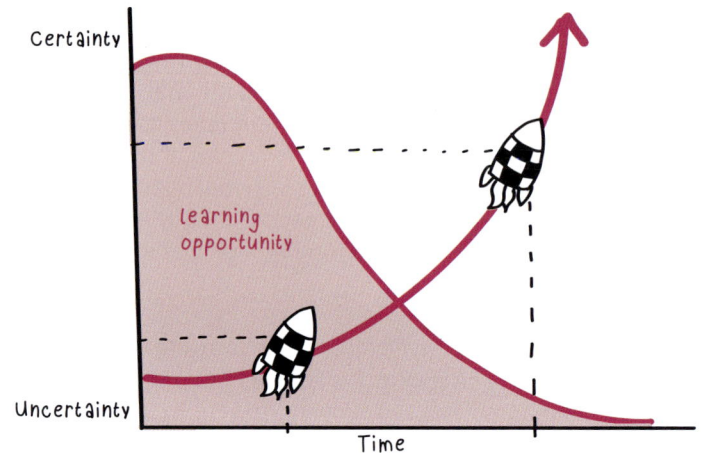

select companies that are backable for a standard investor. Any company whose brilliant scientific or technological solution is offset by lack of business knowledge will have to be declined. If equity is not a factor, you have the option to partner to help a company with it's science or technology as a way to learn, even if you're not thrilled with its business capacity. You could bring a scientific founder with limited business awareness into the accelerator and see what's possible from a business point of view. That could be a huge win for a founder, and a huge learning opportunity for you, with very little loss of opportunity.

Equity amounts for accelerators are fairly standard, between 5–10%. The famous third-party accelerators, Y Combinator and 500 Startups, take roughly 6 or 7%. As a corporate investor, it's best for you to stay in that range—any more and the weight of your brand on the cap table becomes a distraction, any less and the alignment you're seeing becomes too thin, or the amount you can possibly gain becomes too small. Again, you don't *have* to take equity. If you do, it becomes part of the justification for the existence of your accelerator, so choose the amount accordingly.

Consider carefully what you will offer to your startups: In-kind benefits alone, or cash as well? And consider whether or not you'll ask for equity in exchange, and if so, how much.

PHYSICAL PRESENCE: PREPARING YOUR SPACE, EQUIPMENT, AND MATERIALS

You've determined what physical in-kind offerings you'll provide, now let's talk about considerations regarding how you'll deliver those offerings. First, *proximity*. To get the learning benefits your accelerator will drive, you need the day-to-day activities of your accelerator to be located as close as possible to the internal staff who will take on the lessons and insights that ensue. Ideally, you'd be in the same building with the very scientists, technologists, and/or manufacturing leaders who can support and learn from the startups. If you can't find space in a building with relevant staff, can you find space on the same campus? Within easy walking distance? If your accelerator is located far away from where your staff are based, you lose the opportunity for casual and short-notice interaction. You'll need to put more effort into formalizing interactions.

Second, consider *design*. The design of your accelerator space needs to be both functional and appealing. From a functional point of view, you're asking your startups to spend considerable time in this space. You're most effective for their learning and yours (not to mention your relationship) if they come because they see the value, not because you're asking or requiring them to come. They'll only want to come if your space obviously enhances their work more than any other space they can access. If you're giving them lab space, make it great lab space. If you're giving them a cleanroom, make sure it's fully stocked and compliant. If you're offering them prototyping equipment, it should be the same quality you provide to your staff, or better. If in your industry no specialized space is needed and all you have to offer is office/co-working space, make it the best office space they can get—phone booths, conference rooms and snacks. The startup's presence in your physical space is what gives you the opportunity to observe and learn

on a day-to-day basis. If you don't want to offer space, you might be better off with a different type of learning engine with more built-in intimacy, such as a prove-out journey.

In addition to your founders enjoying the space, you also want your staff, external mentors, and ecosystem players to feel magnetized to spend time in your location. Consider colors, furniture style, and decor for a match with your industry's most innovative players while aligning with fundamental cultural considerations. What look and feel will make your partners most likely to want to stop by when they can, on a scheduled or unscheduled basis?

Third, consider your startup partners' *access* and your own *boundaries*. You're likely promising to give them some things—equipment runs, materials and time with your staff. When and where do they get access? Some of these opportunities might be completely free and always available, such as a key card to office space. Others might be limited (they can't call your staff in the middle of the night so no cell numbers), or come with fees (if you're providing hard-to-get supplies that are always available, perhaps they're charged at a discount). It's worth thinking through in advance exactly how you're going to offer what you're offering, and how your boundaries will be embodied.

Location, design, access, and boundary decisions shape the physical activities and behaviors of both startup residents and employees of your firm. How can you maximally encourage their presence and productive interaction?

DECIDE WHAT STARTUPS WILL DO WITH THEIR TIME

The most precious resource startups have is their time. They're limited to the same number of hours in a day as the rest of us, but the stakes, demands, and complexity they face are higher. In order to provide the value exchange you've identified, both your benefits and theirs, you need founders to put in time. Carefully craft your time requests so their effort to build their company and their effort to participate in your accelerator are one and the same. You'll need to decide how long the experience will last, how much actual time your startups will spend during the experience, and what you'll be asking them to do with that time. Keep in mind: No matter how similar your startups are to each other, they're still all at different points along their journey. And also: The more experience your founders have, the less guidance they're likely to want or tolerate. As you make claims on their time, you'll need to make room for the diversity of founder and startup needs.

You'll be selecting startups whose necessary activities match your firm's learning needs. These will be startups who are striving to validate their technologies, business models, markets, and/or investability. Chances are your founders are great scientists or engineers, and/or folks who are passionate about solving a problem with deep personal meaning. The experience that brought them those skills and motives may not have brought them much understanding about how to test the value of a new commercial product. So, you'll need to support their learning process. Many accelerators use a standardized curriculum with weekly events. The more similar your startups in terms of learning stage, the more effective this approach can be. If your startups are at different stages, find a way to customize delivery of validation concepts on an as-needed basis, or face the frustration of founders who don't feel they need what you're teaching. In addition to any curriculum, you'll want to offer individualized time with experts who know the industry, investment patterns, validation practices, and key people who can help the founders move forward. The power of the cohort can be very strong—consider making time each week for founders to share their progress with each other.

How long should your program last? It's common for accelerators to default to a 12-week period. Substantially, that's due to historical reasons (12 weeks is the length of the academic quarter where some accelerator programs were developed), and structural reasons (public companies report results on a

quarterly basis). For some startups, 12 weeks is long enough to learn a great deal and achieve a great deal of validation (think: consumer-facing mobile app), but for most business and industry contexts, you'll have barely gotten to know each other and scratched the surface of possibility. It's best to choose a time period that's suited to communication and sales cycles in your industry, to the amount of intensive learning time you need with each startup, and to the number of cohorts you're looking to run in any given year. We've often seen programs that last up to six months. Merck Digital Sciences Studio companies were in residence for ten months. Add a pre- and/or post-residence component for additional learning.

A cautionary tale: At one startup accelerator we supported years ago, we missed the opportunity to ensure that participating founders wanted the same thing the main firm wanted with regard to time. Some founders gladly accepted the exchange of equity for convertible notes, and went off to spend time pitching their companies to investors, skipping curriculum and opportunities to meet with experts, mentors, and speakers at the accelerator. These founders missed the opportunity to validate their companies and tended to pitch too early, wasting crucial first-impression opportunities. The host firm missed the opportunity to learn from the startups' validation process. During selection, watch for overconfidence or overmaturity on the part of your startups if you want to observe learning. And during the program, make sure every activity you ask your startups to participate in has immediate power in their developmental process. Trust us, if what you're providing isn't useful, your founders will walk.

In short, if you want insight, provide clear and impactful support for your partner's developmental activities. Or, live with whatever they happen to do, whether or not it's relevant for you or even visible to you.

PERSONNEL

Obviously, you'll need a core staff to run your accelerator. At minimum, that will be one full-time equivalent (FTE) leader with business experience and investment awareness in your industry as the main leader. You'll likely need a second FTE who knows the technical side of the work your founders are doing (a scientist or engineer). Part-time admin support is important, especially during more complex periods such as recruiting and onboarding. Naturally, you'll need facilities resources for upkeep.

Beyond the core team, you'll need participation from key internal staff, both to support the startups' learning, and to learn on behalf of the large firm. Luckily, if you're using this book, you've already identified some of the key people through your dashboard alignment work. Now is the time to execute the requests you queued up during your alignment conversations. Lock in commitments from the internal scientists, engineers, business leaders, lawyers, marketers designers, etc., who will be serving, and learning from, your startups.

Tap into the external ecosystem as well. Every investor, lawyer, and other relevant service provider in your region and industry should know what you're doing. Send them newsletters and invite them to major events, for example, a culminating pitch day. Among this cast of characters, partner with your favorites and ask them to support your startups. Ask them to speak at brown bag lunches, provide advisory sessions, offer perks, coach, and consider your startups for investment. Your invitations are likely to be met with enthusiasm, strengthening relationships in all directions. Use your connections to smooth the path for your startups, and for others in the ecosystem who will benefit from those startups. It's very common for accelerators to offer each founder a designated mentor and a stable of experts.

Provide some guidelines: Where and when each role will participate, what they can and can't share, and how they'll report difficulties or insights. Your staff are the face of your accelerator. They deliver the benefits you provide, and draw in the lessons you're hungry to learn. Your setting-up period is the perfect time to attract great talent to run your accelerator.

Running Your Engine
RECRUITING AND SELECTING STARTUPS

We assume you'll be leveraging the marketing muscle of the core firm to get the word out about your accelerator. In addition to usual channels, you'll also invite your internal and external stakeholders to spread the word, announce at relevant conferences and meetups, and use scouting channels, such as Pitchbook, to identify specific startups for outreach. Meet your founders where they are; and give them proper breadcrumbs by which to find you. Make it clear what you're looking for and why you'd be a good partner, so that you're likely to attract the right founders for your goals.

Collect applications through a simple form. Enroll a committee of internal and external stakeholders (why not call on your open innovation squad/advisory board?) to review the applications using a predetermined rubric. You're looking for startups whose journey aligns with your intentions, maturity, and innovation strategy, *and* see you as a particularly well-suited partner, not just a source of cash.

Accelerators are learning engines, so learning is the most important consideration in identifying startups. Perhaps it goes without saying: The best startups for you are those working on questions you need answered. They are focusing on scientific, technological, or business questions you can't answer internally. In order to focus your program and mentor recruiting, you'll likely want to establish a theme or thesis for each cohort.

Innovation framework and the investment differences per stage. *Innovation Accounting*

In addition to suitability of problems to be solved, you also need startups who are at the correct commercial maturity and/or technology readiness level to reveal new information. Startups operate in an uncertain space. By nature, they run into challenges no one could have anticipated. These challenges are just what you wanted to find! Choose startups in the "Goldilocks" zone of maturity—not so early they are busy learning novice lessons about how to run a business, but not so late that they have already addressed all of the uncertainty in the environment and they're just selling products. Of course, it's completely fine to buy products from startups, but that's a different function from your accelerator. The accelerator requires uncertainty to fuel learning—you're bringing in startups specifically because they're exploring an uncertain space.

Consider the direct roles startups might play in your business in the long run. Are you accelerating companies you might want to **acquire** one day? This is a common choice—firms can contribute to the ecosystem by helping startups who can one day become part of the large company's business. There is a trade-off here: If a company joins your acquisition-focused accelerator and is not ultimately acquired, that could weigh on the founder's future chances of success. Their negative experience could result in a negative reputational signal for you. How might you mitigate this?

Alternatively, are you accelerating your **suppliers** to add insight, healthy redundancy, and/or flexibility to your supply chain? An accelerator could allow you to explore future scenarios with new vendors who offer different capacities than your existing vendors, making you more resilient. Path Ahead Ventures, REI's venture arm, includes an accelerator called Navigate that is specifically designed to add diverse perspectives to the shelves at REI. Founders of color are bringing new

ideas that are valuable for REI Members and customers in general—e.g., Mexican home-cooked backpacking meals, and larger sizes for outdoor garments.

Or are you accelerating your **customers**? As they grow, customers learn about markets that matter to you, use more of your products and services, and potentially evangelize on your behalf. Illumina Accelerator took this approach.

Once you know the characteristics of the startups you're looking for, turn your attention to attracting them. As a first principle, be a good partner. If startups join and later discover that you're not a good partner, they'll destroy your reputation in the startup world. Depending on the startup roles you have chosen, you'll need to be an alluring customer, provider, scaling partner, or some combination thereof.

How to be an alluring **customer**: In order to sell products, intellectual property (IP), or the entire company to your firm one day, the startup founder will need to get to know the individuals who can make use of their product or service, as well as the individuals who make the purchase decisions. Giving your founders access to those people can be a huge win for both

sides. Note you are NOT making promises to buy here—you are providing a learning opportunity for both your staff and for the startup. Even if your staff never buys or uses the product, their feedback is invaluable. If you have internal staff who could play this role for a startup, they should be among your dashboard stakeholders, and part of your learning system. To signal that you are a serious *potential* customer worth exploring, reveal how budget decisions are made, and who controls those decisions.

How to be an alluring **scaling partner:** One of the chief reasons startups join accelerators is to take advantage of the scaling infrastructure that large firms enjoy. This is relevant for all categories of startup partners—acquisition targets, vendors, suppliers, customers, etc. How can you address a scale problem for your startup partners? Solve a technology problem with scientific expertise, equipment, materials, and supplies. Solve a space problem with lab, manufacturing, storage, or other specialized space. Solve a connection problem with suppliers, customers, service providers, investors, and other relevant stakeholders. As a large firm, you enjoy a significant presence in the economic ecosystem in your region and industry. How can you leverage this presence on behalf of your startup part-

ners? Solve an information/knowledge problem with business expertise in revenue model, marketing, investment, regulatory, and other key arenas. The more of these challenges you address, the more attractive a partner you become.

Enhance your partner's journey, brand, and cap table. Startup accelerators, overall, suffer from a low-grade reputation because in certain circumstances, accelerator participation has damaged startups, for example, by wasting their time, or inappropriately marking them as "yours" in the open marketplace. Startups experience corporate partnership as both incredibly valuable and rather risky. They consider whether the experience with you will enhance their journey, or damage it. You want founders who consider all of this and choose you because they are confident of the value of your partnership—not partners who accept damage because they are desperate for the money. Let founders know that you'll respect their time by requiring only activities that are immediately valuable and actionable. Promote them in the ecosystem by introducing them to ecosystem players. Publicly celebrate their selection, and invite them to do the same. If you are the startup's customer, say yes when asked to provide letters of intent (LOIs) or other endorsements that honestly demonstrate your interest to their

other stakeholders. And watch for inadvertent handcuffing. Any limits you place on startups' behavior can cause problems for them down the line. If you take rights of first refusal or even first look, this can hurt them with other potential partners. Be sure to understand whether your thumbprint on the startup helps them or hurts them with other potential investors or acquirers, and take action accordingly.

Tell the story of your allure as you market the accelerator opportunity. Your recruiting efforts will call on founders to complete an **application**. We recommend asking for the bare minimum of useful information. Completing the application is one of the first handshakes in your relationship with your partner, so you don't want the process to be onerous. Some obvious things you'll need to know so you can decide which companies are the best match:

89

Startup Accelerator

Information	What You're Looking For
What problem they're solving.	As perfect a fit with your question or theme/thesis as possible.
Status of their solution—most easily expressed in terms of Technology Readiness Level (TRL: use NASA's[2] directly or craft your own).	You're looking for something a bit unfinished so you can watch while they learn. If they're already at 8 or 9, they're likely wrong for the accelerator but could be perfect for your corporate venture capital arm (CVC) or simply for purchase or licensing. The more complex your industry, the less maturity you need—for example, life sciences work is interesting for scientific reasons, right from the beginning. High-tech work might not be interesting until you're trying to sell it to customers.
Manufacturing Readiness Level (MRL). Created by the US Department of Defense, the original MRL[3] offers best practices you can use as a basis. We'll point you to a handy MRL visualization in the endnotes.[4]	Depending on your offerings, your best matches might be companies that can really benefit from your help in the manufacturing design arena, or those who are absolutely ready to run on your machines.
Team's expertise and qualification for roles.	Maturity is unequivocally good here. A seasoned, experienced team working on an early technology, scientific solution, or business model could be ideal for your learning. A less experienced team can still be of interest for your learning, but they'll be less likely to bring you a payoff in terms of the value of your equity.

Once you've reviewed the application you'll want to **interview** your strongest candidates. If you'll be asking them to travel, consider covering their costs, offering a small grant that can make the trip worthwhile for those teams you don't select, or otherwise supporting their travel effort—why drain these small early companies?

In-person interviews are important in the context of an accelerator so that your candidates can review facilities and envision the experience, and so that you can get deeper information about what they'll be working on and how they're likely to go about it. For your part, the goal is to ensure that the work they want to do every day is the work you want to learn from. You can use this information both for selection, and to find the right mentors for selected teams. In-person interviews notoriously exacerbate bias, however. You, like all human beings, evolved to prefer people who are more similar to you, and this happens unconsciously. But the people most like you aren't necessarily the people most suited for your accelerator. Mitigate bias by having multiple interviews, reviewing teams on a rubric, and keeping your most crucial questions consistent across teams. This will give you the best shot at picking well-suited companies.

In addition to reviewing applications and interviewing candidates, you'll also need to review materials. To move quickly limit your interest to the technology/solution (to confirm the TRL and, if appropriate, MRL), the official filings (if you need your teams to have created companies already), and just enough basic financial information to give you confidence that the company will survive your accelerator (noting that you may be infusing some capital). Depending on stage, you may or may not need a sales review. Teams may ask you to sign a nondisclosure agreement (NDA) before they show you their tech, and you may want them to sign an NDA before they start getting advice from your staff.

Now a question that we get asked a lot is how many teams should one select for an accelerator program? Well, the short answer is, that it depends. It depends on your capacity and the set up you decided for. However, typically we see programs of five to ten teams per cohort. Obviously, getting to this number means filtering many more before.

Now that you've found them, what are they actually going to do?

THE PROGRAM

Let's walk through the entire journey from the startup's point of view—starting immediately post-selection.

Before the program begins, establish **expectations**. Who will do what, by when? What are the founders' responsibilities, and what will the accelerator deliver? What contingencies depend on execution on both sides? Articulate this in a formal, signed agreement that covers the exchange of value, term of residence, and any other requirements. You'll also want a bit of ritual, a kickoff event to indicate and elevate the start of the experience. This is the moment where founders meet at least the internal, and perhaps the external, stakeholders who will accompany them on their journey, and where they feel more deeply the honor of having been selected.

During the program, your founders will be present in the accelerator much of the time, and use it as a home base when they're out testing their market (visiting customers, for example). Many accelerators provide and require a **curriculum** that teaches founders how to test their market ideas. It's difficult to craft a set of workshops that's well-timed for companies who are each working on their own separate journeys with their own separate needs. Consider offering learning content such as videos, workbooks, or other broadcast formats so that your founders can use them at the right moment. Ask your mentors to support learning in a bespoke fashion. If you're going to require all teams to attend real-time workshops, they will need to be extremely high-value and immediately actionable. Offer high-quality optional sessions such as brown bag lunches or happy hours with experts.

Advisors, mentors, and coaches from inside and outside your firm play a crucial role. When external, these may be paid experts, or consultants volunteering in order to build a portfolio, or retirees who simply enjoy the work. Internal staff are often called upon to play these roles above and beyond their regular jobs. Your small accelerator team will be responsible for matchmaking and tracking that these conversations are happening.

Advisors	Experts available on a limited ad hoc basis to all teams. May specialize in a particular arena (scientific, business development, etc.), or have very deep knowledge of the industry.
Mentors	Typically, one assigned to each team, with expectations for frequency of meeting.
Coaches	Guides who ensure that the teams have the knowledge and tools they need to complete accelerator expectations, such as reaching a certain number of customers. This role may be played by mentors, or may be a separate paid role with one or two coaches responsible for the cohort.

Your startups will benefit from **relationships with each other**. Their support of and competition with each other can be an important part of the fuel for your program. We recommend a regular group meeting where they can share progress and ask for advice, and an online community where they can participate with each other at will.

Track your teams' progress. The entrepreneurial world has standard ways to talk about startup development, grounded primarily in two factors: Progress raising investment dollars (how many times have they been able to persuade investors to put in how much money?), and progress interacting with the world (how many users have they acquired, how many customers have they acquired and how much revenue have they received?).

Use your curriculum and/or mentors and/or other activities to help them get more investment, and measure their continued investment success. In an accelerator, you help them with investment as a way to serve your founders and the ecosystem on this important goal, thus building up your reputation. The real learning for you occurs as they learn about their market. With regard to revenue, accelerator startups can be extremely early, sometimes starting with just an idea and a strong team, sometimes a prototype, sometimes an unrefined product or service that requires partnership with their customer in order to learn in the field. Help them test the importance of their problem, the value of their solution, and the true basis of their market (e.g., through customer discovery, observation, and ethnographic interviews). Help them build or refine their product, and sign up their first customers. Depending on the cohort, your founders may have similar or different needs, so provide collective or individualized support accordingly.

In order to win the right to continue, you'll need to prove that being in your accelerator is valuable to your firm, to participating startups, and, ideally, to the ecosystem as well. For that reason, you'll need to measure the progress and outcomes of your startups. Measure progress on the factors you're promising to support. Many accelerators use something like the Business Model Canvas to identify specific goals for each founding team. Here's a sample of measures you might track per team:

Investment measures

ACTIVITY
- Progress on the investor deck
- Potential investors contacted
- Investor conversations completed
- Due diligence processes initiated
- Feedback received
- Feedback addressed

OUTCOMES
- Investments closed
- Funding rounds closed

Progress measures

ACTIVITY
- Progress on the design of the customer discovery conversation
- Customers contacted
- Customer discovery conversations completed
- Sales calls completed
- Lessons learned and applied

OUTCOMES
- Sales
- Revenue
- Other indicators relevant for the startup's business model and maturity such as churn rate, customer lifetime value, average cart size, page views, etc.

Why Aren't We Measuring Startup Profits from the Beginning?

If a startup is making profits already, they have their own money to invest. They don't need you as an investor, they probably don't need you for in-kind support, and they probably don't want you involved in their strategy.

If you bring in a company that suddenly starts making a lot of revenue, they should be reinvesting it, not taking it as profit.

You can partner with a profit-generating company, perhaps as a customer (not open innovation) or venture client (counts as open innovation), perhaps a late-stage investment for the CVC—but they don't belong in your accelerator.

In addition to these standard measures of progress, also track how your founders are consuming and learning from your in-kind support: How are they accessing your materials, technologies, customers, etc.? Are they learning to use what you have to offer? Are they taking the actions you expect?

Once the allotted period of time has passed for a given cohort, the program is complete—they've done whatever they were going to do, and you've learned whatever short-term lessons were available. Close your accelerator residency with a culminating event. Typically, accelerator cohorts close with a high-visibility Pitch Day that draws investors, potential customers, and other stakeholders. Spend some time identifying which stakeholders would be most valuable to your founders and to you; and how you might advertise the event to stakeholders you might not know yet. This event provides several benefits:

- Puts your founders and companies on the radar of key stakeholders
- Initiates investment or purchase conversations in the ecosystem
- Attracts internal and external stakeholders to your space
- Provides your founders with a deadline by which to complete a new version of their self-presentation and pitch
- Provides a clearly demarcated end to a chapter of your engagement with the startups
- Elevates the experience with a memorable moment

Develop and run your closing event like any other public corporate event—you likely have internal resources you can draw on to help you execute.

- **Curate** a high-value stakeholder list. Consider both your benefit and your founders'. Invite your contacts who are high-value for the startups, their contacts who might be high-value for you, and new connections you and your founders want to meet.
- Help your founders **prepare** for a great experience. What will they speak about? How will they reference your program? What kind of performance support will you provide in advance (e.g., a pitch or media coach)? Their success during the event is your success.
- **Design and execute** the program thoughtfully. Your C-Suite champion can open the event. The senior accelerator leader can act as MC. Err on the side of interaction—don't ask people to sit and listen too long. Be sure to give your audience plenty of time to meet your founders.
- Ask your founders to provide **testimonials and endorsements** for your accelerator. Closing day is a good time to record your founders' enthusiasm, on a high note!

After your founders "graduate," there is more to learn and more value to create and derive. Stay engaged. Draw on alum founders for advice and resources. As long as you limit the time you ask for, these requests honor your alumni by elevating their experience and expertise. Invite your alumni to meet your current companies. Make advisory matches between your alumni founders and current startups. Record and share their lessons learned.

Keep in touch: Offer a private newsletter with relevant news, events, discounts, and leadership opportunities. Maintain the access paths (email addresses, text numbers and online community access) you created during the program, and attend to requests promptly. You are continuing to burnish your reputation as a good partner. Continue to support alum founders (informally) through contributions like introductions and advice on request, and continue to measure and celebrate their success. And, of course, if you've invested, watch for those investments to ripen over time.

Learning from a Corporate Accelerator

The payoff for your accelerator is learning. Establish up front your practice for acquiring lessons and making use of them. When and where will the staff of your firm be exposed to the lessons startups are learning? Will your staff visit the accelerator on some regular basis? Will certain staffers be assigned to certain startups? Are you hoping your staff will learn from reading reports?

Catch insights directly in the work as your core staff intersect with the startups they are supporting. They may be in a position to make changes in the core business on their own accord, or they may influence changes greater than the scope of their own work. Some examples:

- A startup with a unique technology gets stuck on a technical issue while using your equipment. You find an internal person to help troubleshoot. That person recognizes that the customer support documents could be more clear, and changes them.
- A startup makes a big impact serving a customer you introduced them to. Your sales person references this impact the next time they talk to the same customer.
- A startup hits a major wall in the market and can't find a way around it. You bring this story to your corporate strategy team, and they spin up a project to investigate this wall, or even close off this dead end.
- A startup uncovers a technological solution to a known and important problem. Your firm licenses this solution to increase the value of your products, and raise the price.

Your accelerator staff will catch insights about the accelerator per se, and can make the requisite changes themselves. Given their perspective across the cohort and supporting multiple cohorts, they will also catch insights about the industry. These insights need to be delivered to decision-makers in order to create change.

Measuring a Corporate Accelerator

Above, we wrote about how to measure the progress of your startups. Now let's turn our attention to how you measure and report progress, success, and obstacles for the accelerator engine itself.

As we've said, you'll need to measure the right indicators for each phase of your work. We encourage you to tailor your indicators to your context, using our suggestions as a foundation.

Preparation phase metrics	Operation phase metrics	Outcome phase metrics
• Number of startups applying to your accelerator in a certain unit of time • Number of startups your team has reached out to join your accelerator in a certain unit of time • Conversion rate from applications to enrolled startups • Time it takes to select the startups from the applicants	• Startup-relevant metrics (see metrics in The Program section above) • Number and quality of interactions between startups and mentors, measured through surveys or tracking engagement activities. • Internal resources delivered • Attendance at events • Founder satisfaction (e.g., net promoter score (NPS) • Number of external partners (e.g., other corporates, universities, government bodies, investors and experts) participating in or contributing to the accelerator program • Ecosystem partner satisfaction	• Percentage of accelerator companies that deliver real impact according to the accelerator or cohort theme or thesis (e.g., get integrated into internal processes, shape industry supply chains, etc.). Calculate in comparison to the total number of startups in each cohort, and across all startups over time. • Employee feedback on innovation culture, openness to new ideas, and willingness to collaborate with external entities after the program has run for a reasonable period. • Number of startups from the accelerator program that move into deeper relationships with the corporate (e.g., commercialization pipeline or other open innovation engines). • A financial metric that compares the overall investment made by the corporate partner in the accelerator program to the tangible benefits (including revenue), cost savings, and investment outcomes generated by the implemented solutions. • Change in the valuation of startups post-incubation. This shows how much the market perceives the startups' growth potential and the value of participation in your accelerator.

97

Startup Accelerator

Sunsetting a Corporate Accelerator

Close the accelerator if in practice you're not able to solve the challenges you identified, or when your foundations and positions on the dashboard change to the degree that an accelerator is no longer suitable. Resist closing the accelerator as a knee-jerk move when leadership changes—instead adjust the dashboard in conjunction with the new leader.

The accelerator is an engine that runs in cycles, so if you choose to close it, simply decline to initiate the next cycle. The accelerator team is tiny, so you'll reassign them or (alas) lay them off. You're under no obligation to create fanfare. Take the application down from the web and the sign from the door, redesign or rewrite your web pages as needed, and stop talking about the accelerator. Reinvest your time, capital, and attention into open innovation activities more suited for your stage and industry.

Do please conduct a postmortem to ensure you identify and make use all of the lessons learned! The decision to close the accelerator is significant, and there will certainly be huge learnings. Document these and share them so that a few years down the line another champion knows what you learned and builds on that foundation.

CHAPTER SIX

Startup Incubator

A startup incubator is a physical (usually) base for startups to grind. One decent step up from a garage, the incubator provides space, equipment, access to supplies, and access to expertise and networks, in return (often) for rent. That's right: In a startup incubator, the startups are often glad to pay subsidized rent for offerings that would otherwise be more costly. If you have unused real estate and/or equipment and/or a great network of experts and/or a highly recognized brand in the relevant sector, an incubator can be a great way to dip a toe into open innovation without spending too much. Incubators work best in industries where the resources naturally on offer—space, equipment, supplies, and connections—are truly high-value. If the startup really can do everything from a garage, they don't need an incubator. That means high-resource industries like deep tech, pharma, and med tech are a good fit. In an incubator, your tenants will likely stay with you for at least a couple of years, making for a long-term relationship.

Note: If your assets are already fully occupied by your core business, you won't have excess capacity to rent out. You'll miss out on the efficiency advantage of exploiting otherwise wasted resources. If you're going to spend new money spinning up a partnership engine, you might as well pick an engine with greater outcome potential such as an accelerator, corporate venture capital (CVC), or a prove-out journey.

Your tenants will likely be funded startups who have dollars to pay rent. Incubators generally do not take equity from tenants. That said, Incubators can be a source of ideas and IP for the parent, if you have your stakeholder alignment set up well. Staff from the large organization can spend time with Incubator companies and invite companies of interest to explore part-

nership. Partnership activities are not guaranteed. However, the opportunity for partnership may be part of the value your tenants see for renting from you instead of a neutral space. If partnership is on the table, you'll want to select tenants who are truly potential partners and make sure to move some partnerships forward to demonstrate the possibility.

You might notice that some other authors use the term "incubator" as an umbrella term for all open innovation activity with startups. When we talk about incubators, we're specifically referring to a win–win, landlord–tenant arrangement where the large organization offers low-cost resources that draw startups into proximity, with no particular further obligations.

One of the most famous and longstanding incubators is JLABS,[1] a global initiative of Johnson & Johnson Innovation—JLABS opened its first site in South San Francisco in 2015 and as of this writing is going strong with more than ten global locations. Perhaps one of the secrets to the success of JLABS is that it is one among several engines in Johnson & Johnson's open innovation toolkit, along with strategic partner journeys of various kinds, competitions, ecosystem partnerships, and a serious CVC arm.

Speed to Results

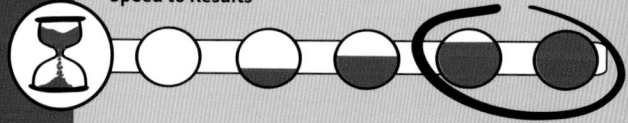

Potential Size of Financial Impact

Scope of Cultural Impact

Visibility

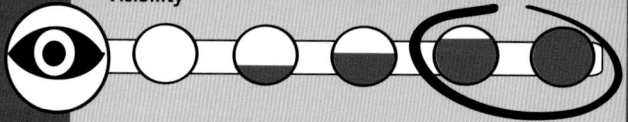

Learning Opportunity

Degree of Corporate Control

Resources Required

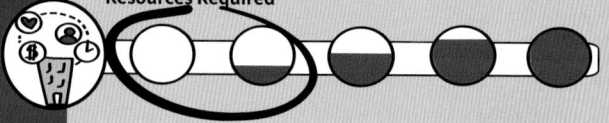

Demand for Speed

Potential Size of Financial Impact

Scope of Cultural Impact

Visibility

Learning Opportunity

Degree of Corporate Control

Resources Required

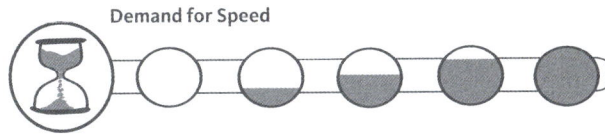

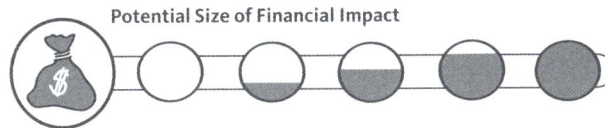

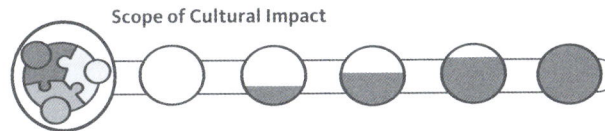

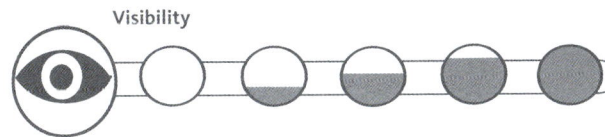

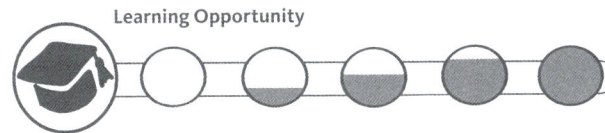

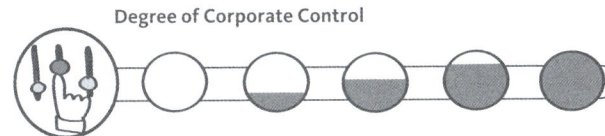

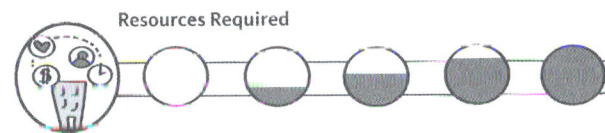

Bend the
back cover flap
over this page
to see your scales
and the Engine's scales
side by side.

Startup Incubator

Incubator Scales

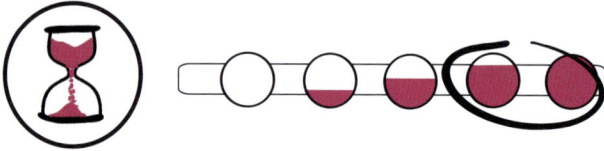

SPEED TO RESULTS:
Revenue as soon as you launch.

An incubator delivers cash immediately after launch, because tenants pay rent. Provided you've read your audience correctly and designed your incubator to suit their immediate needs and budgets, you may not need to wait long for revenue to begin arriving. And if you keep your learning goals modest, whatever lessons may arrive can also begin right away, as soon as the staff of the large firm begins to interact with the tenant startups.

If you need to break even on your external innovation efforts ASAP, an incubator is a good option.

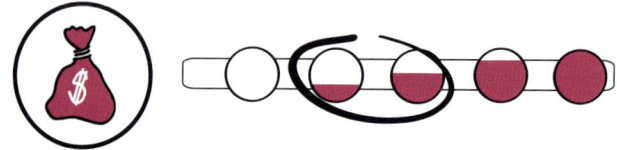

POTENTIAL SIZE OF FINANCIAL IMPACT:
Breakeven, if all goes well.

Rent revenue may serve to offset much or all of the costs of running the incubator. As long as you're careful to use spare real estate, equipment, and supplies, and as long as the incubator isn't responsible for the cost of time of core business staff, your costs remain minimal—mainly a leader, facilities, and administrative support.

You're not taking equity, so any further upside beyond monthly rent will come from partnerships, licensing, or acquisitions that grow out of the incubator. That upside will arrive much later as your tenants move on to other engines, for example, a prove-out journey.

If you can tolerate a relatively low direct investment return (that is, if your open innovation benefits come through visibility and learning more than direct return on investment (ROI)), an incubator is a good choice.

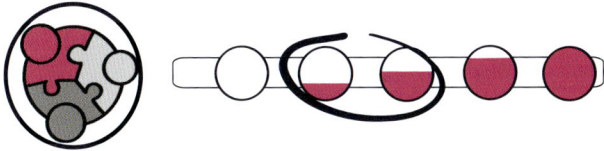

SCOPE OF CULTURAL IMPACT:
Design carefully to increase cultural impact.

The cultural impact of an incubator is entirely dependent on the design of interaction between large-organization core staff and incubator companies. Most incubators require space, and the space offered comes from surplus real estate—this is usually separate housing, with no immediate neighbors from the core staff, and therefore no casual, serendipitous opportunities for cross-pollination between the startups and core staff. You'll have to design opportunities, such as brown-bag lunches, advisory appointments, or lab tours. JLABS has developed a role called a JPAL—a core staff person who champions a startup as they explore partnership. Through this formal responsibility, the JPAL influences the startup and is influenced by it, with a direct effect on the culture. JPAL responsibilities (and honors) are added—over and above the JPAL's everyday scientific, engineering, or business mandate. Therefore, choosing to become a JPAL is itself a cultural act that demonstrates for others how a core staff person can be entrepreneurial. AstraZeneca's Bioventure Hub[2] takes the further step of placing tenants in the same space with the internal Research and Development team (R & D). This proximity dramatically increases opportunities for mutual influence.

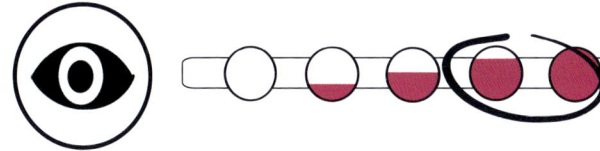

VISIBILITY:
Your incubator needs to be famous.

In order to attract tenants, and in order to attract the other ecosystem players (such as venture capitalists (VCs)) whose presence matters to those tenants, incubators are high-visibility. You'll want an informative and attractive website, a clear application process, significant media and public relations presence, and perhaps glossy brochures.

Choose an incubator when you want attention for your external innovation efforts.

105

Startup Incubator

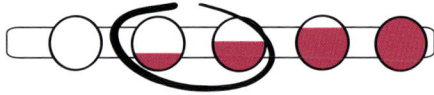

LEARNING OPPORTUNITY:
The chances that you'll learn much are pretty low, but you can design for a better shot.

The startups in an incubator are paying customers. As such, they determine how they spend their time, and how much of it they spend with you. You will certainly learn something about startups in your sector through your marketing campaigns and application process, and you may learn something as your tenants graduate. A formal JPAL-style program or seating the tenants in with internal staff can help you learn more and create a gateway to a more intensive partnership such as prove-out journey, see that chapter below.

An isolated incubator may not be your best path to learning through open innovation. If you choose an incubator for other reasons and you want to learn from it, consider pairing it with other models such as a prove-out journey, CVC, or accelerator.

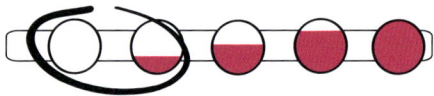

DEGREE OF CORPORATE CONTROL:
Your tenants are completely independent.

A corporate incubator is primarily a landlord. You can ask your tenants to pay on time, clean up after themselves, and be good neighbors to their fellow tenants. You can't control anything at all about their business, even whether or not they make use of

your staff as mentors. Your startups are your customers and you serve at their pleasure.

If you want an open innovation effort that is primarily observational, if daily co-location with startups is enough opportunity for you, an incubator is a good choice.

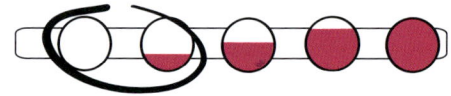

RESOURCES REQUIRED:
Spare capacity keeps your costs low.

Corporate incubators are among the least costly of open innovation engines, as they are designed to work with spare capacity—space you already own or lease but can't or choose not to fill with core work, equipment you make or own in excess of your needs, etc. You can operate with a fairly skeletal crew: You will need an experienced leader who understands the sector from a business point of view and is well connected in the ecosystem, a scientist or engineer who understands the equipment well, and administrative/facilities staff time. Much or all of this cost may be offset with rents.

If you need to keep your open innovation costs low, a startup incubator may be suitable.

Why Should You Choose This Engine?

A startup incubator is a great way to make use of stranded or underused assets. You bring in rents, potentially enough to break even on the costs of your space, materials, equipment, and supplies. You develop magnetism in your entrepreneurial ecosystem by hosting the investors and service providers your partners need to meet. You'll shine up your brand's innovativeness credentials. And you open the possibility of compelling business opportunities: The very presence of startups conducting business and research from inside your building means that you'll be just a few steps away when discoveries are made. Design your incubator right and you can use it to drive highly productive partnerships down the line. If you're in a complex industry where founders need space and equipment that are expensive or hard to come by (think biosciences or advanced materials), you'll be very attractive and can select from among the best partners in the industry.

Why Shouldn't You Choose This Engine?

An incubator by itself is unlikely to transform the large organization or lead to major discoveries. And if you lack spare assets, creating an incubator is going to cost you. Another consideration: Not every industry needs space, equipment, or materials. If the startups in your industry can operate completely on their own from a suburban basement or garage, they won't benefit from your incubator—the strongest founders simply won't come. A mobile app designer who needs an incubator is likely very early in their process and therefore lacking in funds to pay rent. Don't build an incubator if you don't have the resources to solve immediate needs for strong founders in your industry.

Making a Startup Incubator Work

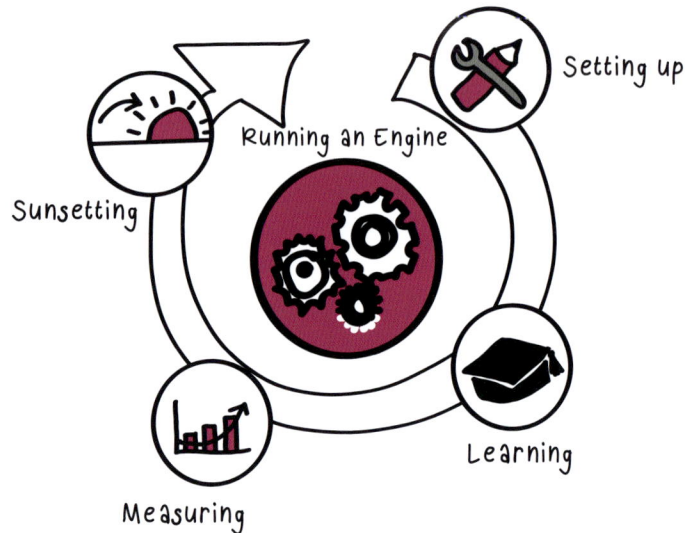

Running an Engine

Setting up

Sunsetting

Learning

Measuring

You've identified the incubator as a key engine for your open innovation effort. That means you plan to make assets (ideally underutilized ones you already have on hand) available to startups, possibly for a fee, and it means you're not taking any equity. Since you're reading about incubators in a book about open innovation, it's clear you also intend to take advantage of the startups' proximity to your organization and a relatively long-term relationship (two or three years) as a way to learn. Therefore, in addition to setting up and maintaining space and equipment, and in addition to attracting startup tenants, you'll also need a way to bring insights and partners into the main organization. Let's step through it.

Setting Up Your Incubator

Startups join an incubator primarily because it's the best way to get their work done. They value subsidized access to resources and they value future partnership opportunities as well, but getting work done is primary. So, the focus in setup is to make sure you're identifying the right assets, setting the right rent, and staffing so that all goes smoothly. You might also offer some optional activities.

PHYSICAL PRESENCE

Ideally, the assets underpinning your incubator are ones you have already acquired for the purposes of your main business (e.g., lab space, manufacturing equipment and customer lists). Your task is to choose assets that are enormously valuable to startups who might find them difficult to access at any cost. These same exact assets might represent sunk costs for you, so they're very inexpensive from your point of view. Why this focus on unused or underutilized sunk-cost assets? It's crucial that you keep your costs low: In this context, you're not taking equity so there's no big risk that could generate a big reward. You can't justify costs on the basis of the opportunity for huge equity wins.

What will your space look like? You'll want to create a warm and engaging home for your founders. You'll want them to feel safe, so they'll need good security on their systems and a place to lock their sensitive items. At the same time, you need access so you can learn. So, for example, if what you're offering is lab space you'll prefer to provide workbenches in an open lab with

shared equipment (rather than, say, private, locked rooms). In addition to the workspace, you'll also need a way to host the ecosystem—perhaps that's a large open space somewhere else on the site, or perhaps you can make room by moving equipment.

Promise your tenants enough time with your firm's staff to make future partnership possible, but limit your staff's demands on founders' time and vice versa. The directors of the BioVenture Hub have found that internal staff are eager to spend time with founders.

DETERMINE THE RENT

You can't charge startups very much, they simply don't have the cash (yet). So why charge them at all? There are two reasons to charge, and both can help you determine an appropriate rate. First, the rent can help to offset any remaining costs that go beyond the loose real estate and equipment you're providing—staffing, advertising, etc. So, consider these costs and what they would look like divided across your incubator companies. You may or may not be able to reach pure breakeven, but you can certainly balance out some of your costs.

Second, charging rent drives founders to show up. Founders live under investor scrutiny and therefore are very careful with cash. When they give up a monthly fee, they will feel obligated to justify that fee by using what they've paid for. They will show up in the lab, they will plan runs on your equipment, etc., and that's what you need for your learning. If you don't charge any rent, founders may not feel any particular obligation to be present on any regular basis. As you may have seen when you host events: Complimentary tickets are often not used. Charge enough that founders feel the burn.

The most important consideration when it comes to setting fees is market rate. Your charges to startups need to feel subsidized relative to the open market for the same assets—that's a primary reason why they'll choose you. In a market where

these assets are hard to come by, you can come close to market rate because it's a win to access them at all. Similarly, if proximity to your brand is extremely high-value, you might be able to demand a higher rent. Do keep in mind that the incubator is not itself a profit-making business. You're reducing the cost of otherwise wasted assets and bringing in any learnings and partnership opportunities—spend your time on those considerations and not on perfecting your price.

PERSONNEL

Operationally, you need *an incubator leader* with business and technical credibility—this person attracts startups and ecosystem players, and acts as a liaison to the main business. You need *a scientist or engineer* to guide founders in using the assets, if assets are provided. You need *facilities staff* to make sure things work smoothly and look good. And you need *an administrator* who handles payments and issues. You might also need *an event coordinator* from time to time.

In order for your organization to learn from the incubator, you need time from your core business staff—scientists and engineers who can help founders and learn from them regarding the invention itself, and guides who can connect founders with decision-makers in the organization when deeper decision opportunities arise. For example, Johnson & Johnson Innovation's JPALs are internal staff tasked with looking for Johnson & Johnson business opportunities for founders, along with their regular duties.

And in order to learn together about the ecosystem around your founders' technologies, including investment appetite, customer needs, supply chain, etc., you and your founders need outside voices. Engage mentors from the external ecosystem and partner with service providers. An additional benefit of engaging outside resources is the increased value to your tenant companies.

Running Your Engine
RECRUITING, SELECTING, AND ONBOARDING STARTUPS

You're offering important assets, so it shouldn't be difficult to attract more founders than you can serve, nor will it be difficult to find the right places to advertise the opportunity—hopefully you're already participating in your ecosystem (see the earlier chapter on the Open Innovation Ecosystem) to know where your founders are spending their time. Even though you are charging rent, it's still appropriate to be selective. This is open innovation, not simple landlording, so you need companies who are working at the right stage on questions that interest your firm, and you need companies whose activities enhance, or at least don't harm, your brand. Provide an application, a site visit, and an interview where you and any given founder can size each other up. Your application, evaluation rubric, and review committee (perhaps drawn from your dashboard stakeholder team) should be driven by strategic intent from the core business. What is the core business looking for in terms of technologies, services, partners, or insights? The more input and participation you can get from the core business, the better for your chance of absorbing discoveries for business impact, and the better for your chance of generating deeper partnerships down the line. Of course, you'll also want some confidence that your tenants will be able to pay your fee and last long enough to generate the learning you're after.

When companies are selected and choose to join, you'll provide a standard rental agreement, and include expectations about access to mentors, service-level expectations for equipment, mutual nondisclosure, and on the founder's part: Demonstration of forward motion. You'll also need to establish trust. Your founders are letting you in to their business without any equity exchange to keep the two entities in alignment. How will your tenants know that you'll treat their information honorably? You'll need both formal language in the agreement, and consistently appropriate behavior.

When each firm arrives, you'll provide orientation, equipment, and safety training, a welcome gift, a community introduction, and any other appropriate entry rituals to establish the culture of your incubator. Decide: Will you start by filling your incubator and open individual slots as companies "graduate"? Will you keep some space inventory open in order to offer waves of admissions?

DAY-TO-DAY ACTIVITY IN THE INCUBATOR

In running an incubator, you are serving founders as your tenants. Your first responsibility is to ensure that your resources are functioning as expected—equipment maintenance, cleaning, etc. Your second responsibility is to disturb or obligate them as little as possible. So there's no required curriculum to attend. At the same time, housing founders together in a single location brings significant opportunities. Bring in relevant scientific, engineering, and business experts for brown-bag lunches and mentorship. On a regular basis (quarterly?) host events with key ecosystem players such as investors and service providers. Maintain lists of interested ecosystem players and provide introductions generously. Invite staff from the parent firm to visit, mentor, and (where appropriate and mutually desired) collaborate with your startup founders. These activities should be so valuable that founders choose to engage as much as possible.

"GRADUATING" INCUBATOR COMPANIES

Your tenants may one day outgrow your space—when the scale of their experiments or number of employees grows too high, they'll move on. In the San Francisco Bay Area in Life Sciences, Diana has noted that this happens pretty rarely. The value of lab space is extremely high, and tenants like to stay who stops progressing may no longer be a fit. Set up a progress evaluation process by which teams inform you about their forward motion with regular cadence. It's important that they get value from this conversation, so the person receiving this information needs to be a credible mentor, connector, or incubator leader. This same exact process is an important element of your learning function (see the section just below on learning from a startup incubator). If you and the startups agree, you might use measures similar to those outlined for evaluating startup progress in the Accelerator chapter above.

When you recognize that a company is no longer a fit for your organization, let them know you won't be renewing at the end of the current term, and help them find their next location. Sometimes, good parents have to kick fledglings out of the nest—do so with encouragement, kindness, connections, and a way to stay connected as an alum. That's different from evicting a nonpaying or rule-breaking tenant—you might have to do that once in a while too.

When you recognize that a company has validated its market and/or technology enough to deepen the partnership, consider investing through a CVC, partnering through a prove-out journey (including, perhaps, becoming an early customer to the startup), or admitting the company into a higher-touch acceleration program. You might even license their product or consider them for an acquisition.

When a tenant itself decides to move on, wish them well and support them.

Create an offboarding checklist for smooth handover of keys, a closing ritual akin to graduation, and an alumni program that brings alumni back as mentors and learners. That way any tenant in good standing leaves with good will and stays in the ecosystem.

a long time. We've seen incubators that simply maintain a tenant–landlord relationship: As long as the founder pays rent and follows house rules, they can stay. This can be great for keeping assets in use, but it's not very good for the learning component of open innovation. You need a way to bid farewell to some teams on a regular basis so that you can bring in new ones. You need a way to know when a team is no longer generating enough insight for your firm. You might want to use the incubator as a pipeline to other engines, such as a prove-out journey, accelerator, or CVC. So, you'll need a way to understand your tenants' progress, and a stated term (time period) in the rental agreement.

As long as you're clear up front, you can require teams to move forward on their own goals in order to maintain their status. Through your selection process, you've ensured that your tenants are working on questions of interest to you. Any team

Learning from a Startup Incubator

Your tenant companies are completely independent, with no obligations to you apart from paying rent and making progress. So, how will you get enough exposure to learn? The answer is to provide support and advice. Your founders will be eager to talk to your engineering, scientific, and business staff and show them work *to the extent those interactions are valuable for the founders*. And to the extent you have established trust through your agreement and good-neighbor behavior.

There are several channels by which to learn from the companies in your incubator: *First*, through interaction with your scientific/technical incubator staff—in progress evaluation/feedback sessions (see the "graduating" section just above), or ad hoc in the day to day. *Second*, through interaction with visiting staff from the parent company, whose mentoring conversations may reveal interesting findings about markets or tech. *Third*, through ecosystem activity such as the questions founders ask or answers they give at brown-bag lunches, the introductions they ask for and what you hear back about those introductions, or at events organized by the incubator. *Fourth*, through day-to-day activity such as the amount of consumable materials they go through in a given week.

Insights may come through success/failure metrics, consumption/ production metrics, or stories about technical, business, and inter- personal experiments (the attempts that don't work are usually the most interesting). Deliver your learnings to the person most able to make use of them. Core parent company staff might get their learning directly as they walk alongside your founders. You should also catch insights of significant relevance to business or technical leaders who don't participate directly. Deliver these through regu- lar reports, newsletters, or on an as-discovered basis, tuned to your particular firm's needs.

Track your learnings and use them to justify continued incubator activity, as well as to know when any given company stops produc- ing relevant learnings for you (see the "graduating" section above).

Measuring a Startup Incubator

As always, we encourage you to tailor your indicators to your context. Use our suggestions as a foundation upon which you can build further:

Preparation phase metrics	Operation phase metrics	Outcome phase metrics
• Number of startups applying to your incubator in a certain unit of time • Number of startups your team has reached out to to join your incubator in a certain unit of time • Time it takes to select tenants from the applicant pool	• Startup-relevant metrics (e.g., experiments completed, regulatory steps completed, customer outreach progress and funding raised—will vary by industry) • Cost of the incubator per startup per month • Number and quality of engagements between corporate teams and startups, including workshops, mentoring sessions, and joint development efforts • Number and quality of interactions between startups and mentors, measured through surveys or tracking engagement activities (providing that your incubator offers access to mentorship) • Founder satisfaction (e.g., Net Promoter Score (NPS)) • Ecosystem partner/mentor satisfaction	• Change in the valuation of startups post-incubation. This shows the market's perception of the startups' growth potential. • Founder and ecosystem partner/mentor satisfaction • Number of business partnerships or collaborations that startups form during the incubation period, in particular partnerships with business units from your company • Tenants' business success post-incubation relative to their business model (e.g., ROI, social impact, revenue, CLTV, etc.) • Cost-benefit analysis of the incubator relative to leaving the assets un-utilized.

Sunsetting a Startup Incubator

If you decide to close your incubator, you'll need to provide time for your tenant founders to move. Your rental agreement will specify move-out times and requirements. Let your ecosystem community know you're shuttering your doors, what you learned, and what you're doing next. It's imperative that you document your learning—not only the specific insights that emerged from each tenant company, but also what you learned from developing the incubator in the first place. How much did you save by using resources that would otherwise go to waste? What intended and unintended ripple effects did the presence of your incubator cause in your ecosystem? What did you discover about the market for your resources, and about the markets in which your tenants operated? Document these past insights so that you take advantage in the present, and avoid repeating any mistakes in the future.

7

CHAPTER SEVEN

Corporate Venture Capital

Corporate venture capital (CVC) is a highly popular approach to corporate innovation: This is the large organization's take on traditional venture capital (VC) funding, supplying capital in exchange for equity. Acting as an investor in the ecosystem is a powerful choice. As a literal capitalist, your firm becomes a magnet for startups with technologies, services, or business models tied to your industry. Your special domain expertise makes you an especially attractive partner and may make you especially good at spotting good investments.

CVC arms are often, but not always, created as separate entities with independent balance sheets. This separation simplifies taxes and walls off the ups and downs of venture capital from the main firm's quarterly reporting to shareholders. CVCs always have two goals: One goal is financial, and the other is strategic.

The financial goal is straightforward, and similar to traditional VC—make money directly from investment as the value of each investment increases and is eventually sold. By investing in startups that, if successful, could become hugely valuable, CVCs give their parent companies a shot at significant return.

Strategic goals are in the direct interest of the future of the parent business: For example, ecosystem building, brand visibility, environmental/social impact, or filling the technology pipeline. One significant strategic goal is learning: Strategic CVCs participate in the capital market in the relevant sector in order to understand what's happening from a business, customer, and/or technology

point of view. The presence of the strategic goal brings powerful in-kind assets into play. Far better than traditional VCs, CVCs can help their portfolio companies with technical knowledge, specialized equipment, materials, customer pipelines, supply chain support, etc.

A CVC that is primarily strategic limits its investment appetite to strategically relevant companies. A CVC that is primarily financial can explore more broadly but may provide less learning value along the journey. Generally speaking, CVCs carry both goals but lean more heavily into one.

If you're running multiple open innovation engines simultaneously, the CVC's scouting effort can benefit all: The CVC takes a huge number of startup meetings, and some candidates deemed not appropriate for direct investment may be well-suited to other partnership opportunities such as accelerators (see that chapter above), prove-out journeys (see that chapter below) or licensing.

CVCs, like traditional VCs, invest in a portfolio of companies. Theoretically, according to the power "law", one giant success covers any losses from startups that fail to reach a high-multiple exit.

Venture investments are intentionally high-risk, high-reward relative to other forms of investing. Assets (the startups) are selected for investment on the chance that they could provide a truly outsized return, which can only happen with a hugely impactful and very new technology and/or business model Hugely impactful and very new technologies (and business models) are by nature very uncertain. Technology and market

obstacles prevent most startups from reaching significant success. But a few do succeed on a massive scale. As Peter Thiel famously put it in Zero to One, "*The biggest secret in venture capital is that the best investment in a successful fund equals or outperforms the entire rest of the fund combined.*"[1] This principle is known as "the power law." Venture capitalists have come to expect that most individual investments will lose money, break even, or make a slight profit, while a few will pay off at a level orders of magnitude above the original investment.[2]

CVC investments tend to exit more frequently than traditional VC, perhaps because the CVC can provide significant in-kind support. Even so, chances are most of the startups in the portfolio will not provide much of a return.[3] The overall ROI comes from a few real winners.

Like VCs, CVCs help their portfolio companies succeed through a significant investment of dollars, as well as providing advice and making connections. Because CVCs are tied to the parent company, at least by name, they may be able to offer resources that traditional VCs can't—this includes brand connection and might also include specialized expertise, equipment, customer lists, etc.). Some CVCs join the startup's business as board observers or acting board members.

Startups may be more or less interested in CVC investment depending on how they perceive the large firm's brand or partnership reputation.

Here's how CVCs stack up on the scales.

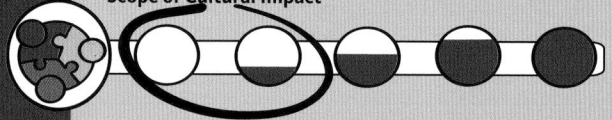

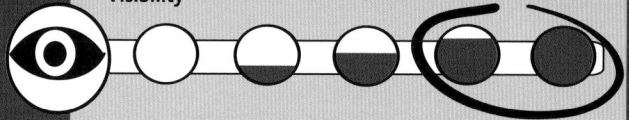

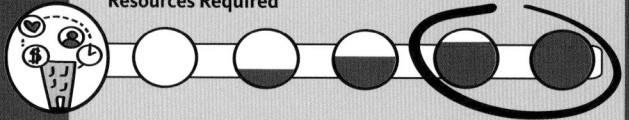

Demand for Speed

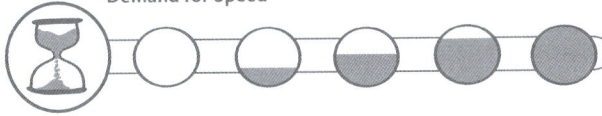

Potential Size of Financial Impact

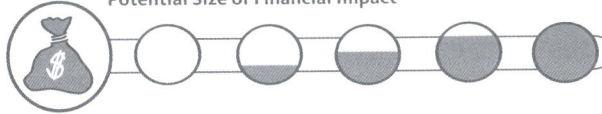

Scope of Cultural Impact

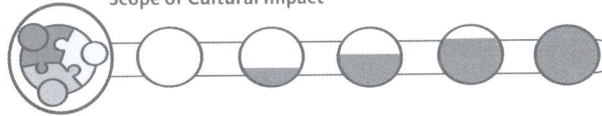

Visibility

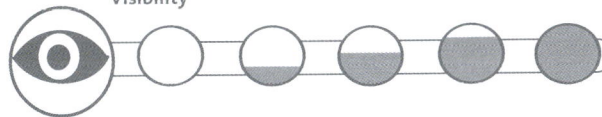

Learning Opportunity

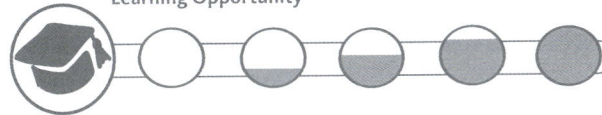

Degree of Corporate Control

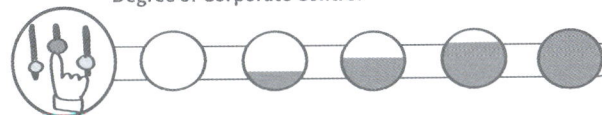

Resources Required

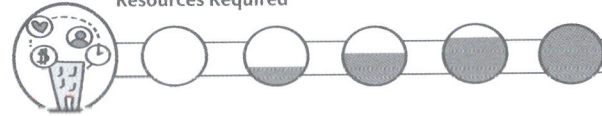

Bend the
back cover flap
over this page
to see your scales
and the Engine's scales
side by side.

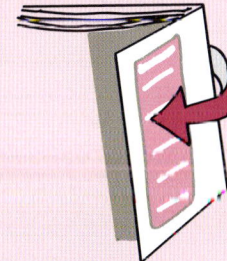

Corporate Venture Capital Scales

SPEED TO RESULTS:
Return on investment (ROI) arrives after exit.

How long you'll wait for results for a CVC depends on which goals you're emphasizing. Strategic goals begin to pay off immediately, whereas financial goals can take three, five, or ten years or more depending on the industry. That's because the ROI typically arrives when the startup "exits"—becomes a public company, or is purchased. That's when the stock can be sold for a high multiple.

A CVC is a good fit for organizations whose open innovation initiatives have a few years of grace before needing to demonstrate financial results.

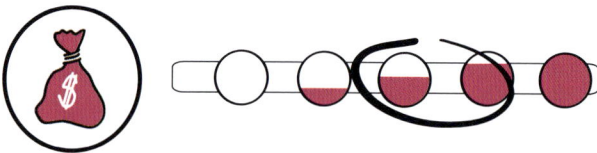

POTENTIAL SIZE OF FINANCIAL IMPACT:
ROI could be significant, Potentially.

Relative to other partnership engines, CVC activities wield substantial potential for influencing the financial profile of corporations. By strategically investing in high-financial-potential external startups at a sufficiently early stage, corporations not only gain access to cutting-edge technologies and novel business models but may also reap considerable financial rewards

if all goes well. Successful CVC initiatives can lead to lucrative exits through acquisitions or initial public offerings (IPOs), providing a substantial ROI.

One notable example of how CVC can result in high financial impact is Google Ventures' investment in the ride-sharing pioneer, Uber. In 2013, Google Ventures participated in a significant funding round for Uber, marking a strategic move to align with the innovative disruptions occurring in the transportation industry. This investment not only provided Google with a foothold in the burgeoning sector but also contributed to Uber's rapid expansion. Eventually, Uber's valuation soared, making it one of the most valuable startups globally. When Uber went public in 2019, Google Ventures (rebranded as GV) realized a twenty-fold return on its initial investment—in the span of only six years.[4] Note that Uber showed a profit for the first time in 2023!

The success of this CVC initiative not only yielded significant financial gains for Google but also showcased the strategic prowess of CVC in identifying and supporting disruptive technologies that can redefine industries and create substantial value for both the invested company and the corporate investor. Another concept showcased in this story: If you're able to make a very substantial investment, CVC, like VC in general, can be somewhat self-fulfilling: By investing, you put a great deal of energy behind an idea. Ideas in which you do not invest do not receive that energy.

That said: It's important to be aware that successes like the Google story are rare. Even in highly successful CVC endeavors, most individual CVC-backed startups do not provide a huge payoff.[5] It's also worth noting that the relationship between CVCs and their investees can be complex.[6] The Google/Uber story itself went sour due to intellectual property (IP) and staffing disputes even before the exit. Perhaps all parties went crying to the bank—this type of tension doesn't need to be a showstopper, it's just something to be prepared for.

If your organization is very keen on financial impact from open innovation, is willing to risk some capital up front, and can stand the heat of high-stakes partnerships, consider creating a CVC arm.

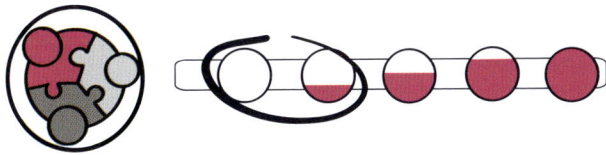

SCOPE OF CULTURAL IMPACT:
Not much impact on the main organization from CVC activities.

Typically, CVC groups operate externally to the core organizational structure—in fact quite often they are created as completely separate organizations with separate premises and balance sheets. That's because the balance sheet of a CVC looks volatile: Large amounts of money go out in a short period of time (investment). Then nothing happens for a long time while the investments develop. Ultimate profits and losses arrive over years, not over quarters. Tax planning can also drive large organizations to keep the CVC as a separate entity. When the CVC is separate, there is little or no interaction between the staff of the CVC and the staff of the main organization, and therefore little or no impact on culture.

Even when not formally separated, the work, expertise, goals, and timelines of the CVC staff are very different from the core work of the parent company. These differences make it unlikely that the CVC will impact the culture of the parent company in any significant way. With extensive work to ensure cultural ties, it would be possible to create a cultural influence, but not without investing additional time and money into this function.

While CVCs can contribute valuable external perspectives, networks, and tech-awareness, their influence on the deeply ingrained cultural aspects of the organization is likely to be limited. Any small influence will arrive through the sheer pride in association with a CVC, through leadership communications to employees, or through staff members who are called upon to assess or advise the investments.

Choose CVC if you're happy with your core culture, or if you're happy to address cultural concerns in a different way.

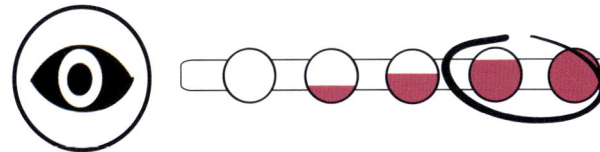

VISIBILITY:
Your CVC needs to be famous.

CVC arms are highly visible in their nature. To attract investible startups, CVCs need to put themselves squarely in the spotlight within the startup ecosystem. By doing so, they also make themselves highly visible to shareholders, employees, competitors, and customers. If you want everyone to know you're involved in open innovation, establishing a CVC is a good way to catch their eye. As with a startup accelerator, the marketing of your CVC is inherently the marketing of your organization's commitment to innovation, collaboration, and staying at the forefront of trending technologies and business models.

CVC can serve as a compelling and impactful open innovation engine for organizations keen on public interest and attention. If you're not keen on public interest and attention, choose a different engine.

121

Corporate Venture Capital

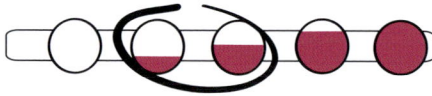

LEARNING OPPORTUNITY:
CVC learning can be compelling but limited.

Establishing a CVC arm can certainly yield valuable insights for your company by forcing attention to the experience of specific startups as they attempt to impact an industry. However, the depth of these learnings may be limited. This limitation stems from the fact that CVCs usually live outside the core of the company, so it's a challenge to drive insights into organizational strategy. In addition, the CVC's view inside of its portfolio company is somewhat limited. Depending on the size of investment, you may have an opportunity to observe or even guide at the board level, but you may not be invited into the lab, onto the manufacturing floor, or into the business design conversations.

If your organization prioritizes extensive learning as a core objective in its open innovation, consider alternative approaches that offer more direct and profound knowledge exchange.

DEGREE OF CORPORATE CONTROL:
Your money buys a bit of control.

In a CVC arrangement, the CVC and the startup are partners, with separate swim lanes. The CVC supplies dollars and the startup attempts to turn those dollars into commercial success. The large organization doesn't get to make decisions on behalf of the startup. That said, as a financial partner who might invest, acquire, or purchase solutions further in the future, the CVC has significant influence delivered through various types of in-kind assistance including strong advice. Depending on the size of the investment, the CVC may place a staff person on the startup's board, typically as a nonvoting observer.

A CVC is a good option for your organization if you want some influence on your startup partners and value their independence at the same time.

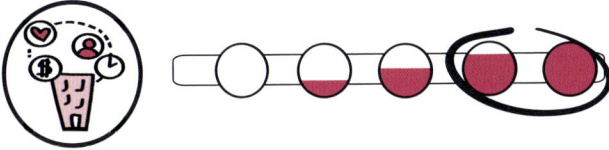

RESOURCES REQUIRED:
Plan for a significant resource investment in return for the reward opportunity.

Engaging in CVC constitutes a money-intensive endeavor, with the primary emphasis on financial resources rather than other forms of support. The size of a CVC budget can vary widely and is influenced by factors such as the objectives of the CVC, the industry, and the scale of the parent company. CVC budgets typically range from tens of millions to several hundred million dollars.[7] Some large corporations allocate significant resources to their CVC activities, allowing them to make substantial investments in startups and emerging technologies. The budget size depends on the risk appetite and financial capacity of the company, as well as the specific goals it aims to achieve through its CVC initiatives. The budget for CVC is a strategic decision based on the company's overall investment strategy and its commitment to fostering innovation and growth.

For instance, Intel Capital, the VC arm of Intel Corporation, was the first and perhaps most prominent CVC player. Founded back in 1991, Intel Capital has managed funds in the range of hundreds of millions to over a billion dollars. For example, in 2020 alone, they invested between $300–500 million dollars in promising technology companies.[8] Intel Capital's significant budget has allowed it to make numerous investments in startups and emerging technologies across different sectors, showcasing the substantial financial commitment that some corporations allocate to their CVC initiatives.

CVC serves as an excellent open innovation mechanism for companies that are comfortable with financial risk and have the financial capacity to support such endeavors.

Why Should You Choose this Engine?

Through CVC, a large organization gains access to external innovation, cutting-edge technologies, and disruptive business models by investing in startups. This not only diversifies the organization's business but also fosters strategic partnerships, potentially leading to collaborations or acquisitions that strengthen market positions.

Moreover, CVC activities offer valuable market insights and enhance the company's agility by staying attuned to dynamic industry trends. Beyond the business benefits, a CVC arm can attract entrepreneurial talent, contribute to talent retention, and position the company as an innovation leader, conferring a competitive advantage. As we've seen with Intel, CVCs can even shape markets and industries with enough investment and patience.

While financial gains are not the sole focus, successful CVC initiatives can yield profitable exits, further solidifying the company's position in the market. Overall, building a CVC arm aligns with a forward-thinking approach, positioning the company for sustained success in a rapidly evolving business landscape.

Why Shouldn't You Choose this Engine?

CVC initiatives demand significant financial resources and the ability to lay out cash for an extended period of time while investments mature. Investing in startups entails significant risk at the level of individual decisions. Given the power law (see above), CVCs aggregate a portfolio of investments in the hope that at least one will do well, and there's no guarantee. Don't build a CVC if you can't make the case for risk to your stakeholders.

The external and independent nature of CVCs can also pose challenges in integrating their activities with the company's core operations, potentially leading to lost learning opportunities, or worse, cultural clashes and strategic misalignment.

Managing a CVC effectively requires specialized skills and expertise, and companies lacking experience in venture investing may find it challenging to navigate the complexities of the startup ecosystem. This can be addressed by hiring outside expertise. However, the outside expert may not understand the corporate environment in general or your organization in particular.

Key reasons why corporate venture arms fail:

- Putting a short-term focus on this long-term investment engine. Venture investments require years to deliver financial results – quarterly evaluation is a lethal mismatch.
- Insufficient budget commitment. Effective CVC requires a broad portfolio and risk-taking
- Insufficient training of key stakeholders (CVC leaders and internal executives).[9]

Making Corporate Venture Capital Work

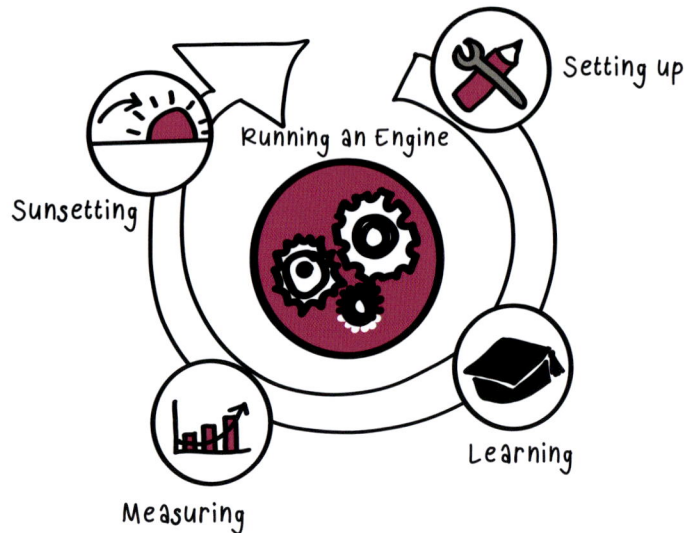

Running an Engine
Setting up
Sunsetting
Learning
Measuring

VC (traditional and corporate) provides cash to commercialize technologies that could not otherwise move forward. You can make a huge difference to a small company with a relatively small dollar investment. In spite of its popularity as an open innovation engine,[10] setting up a CVC is not an easy endeavor. Many companies have fallen into the trap of assuming that the CVC is the easiest open innovation engine to set up, or that CVCs deliver success like magic. It's a bit more complicated than that.

Setting Up Your Corporate Venture Capital
DECIDE WHERE YOUR CORPORATE VENTURE CAPITAL ACTIVITY WILL RESIDE

Your CVC journey starts with a significant decision: Whether the CVC will reside inside or outside your company. Here, there are three paths you can take: Create a new legal entity, invest from internal funds, or join a traditional VC as a limited partner (LP).

One popular route is for your company to set up its own VC fund, creating **a new legal entity** that is dealing solely with investing in startups. The fund will be administered by a general partner (GP) which operates the newly created entity, and it will have one single LP, which is the parent company.

Why create a CVC fund separate from the main company? First, it helps with your company's accounting, containing the risk, tax implications, and market operations associated with the investment in startups in a separate legal entity. Then, it's about focus and flexibility: Employees working under this separate legal entity will have more freedom to scout for startups and take investment decisions than if they were directly under the corporate umbrella—that's because their incentives are tied directly to the success of the CVC, and not subject to the constraints of the mothership. Finally, in terms of managing the investments made, having a separate fund will make day-to-day operations smoother and fit to purpose.

But a stand-alone CVC fund comes with real challenges. One factor is that it takes time to kick your investment activity into gear as you gather the needed capital, assemble a team of investment pros, create the governance, and set up the new legal entity. Another concern is that if the CVC is a separate entity, there will be firewalls between the core business and the investment activity, reducing the fidelity of lessons learned and making any hand off of discovered technologies more difficult.

Another approach to the setup of your CVC is to **invest from internal funds**, perhaps creating a department responsible for this function. This has the advantage of more control and easier access, as well as potentially a shorter path to getting started. Your learning opportunity can be very high as you construct direct relationships between your startups and your firm. However, in this setting, investments appear directly on your books, with tax implications for success and potential stock price implications for failures. You also carry company and regulatory policy considerations directly into the CVC's work.

If your company is eager to enter the CVC world but neither of the options above seem right or are likely to be approved by the board just yet, there is a third option available: **become an LP in an external CVC** alongside other LPs. The CVC is managed and administered by an experienced third party whose only responsibility is to the well-being of the fund. Upon becoming an LP, the corporation gains swift and convenient entry to deal flow, allowing investments in sectors that extend beyond the core business. In this arrangement, the corporation depends on the VC fund to handle investment decisions efficiently. However, this setup comes at the cost of diminished influence and autonomy over investments, offering fewer scouting and trend insights and opportunities for the corporation. Moreover, as an LP, the corporation faces restricted access to information concerning the day-to-day operations of the portfolio companies. This approach is hassle-free and potentially less risky for your company, but it comes at the expense of learning, for example, regarding technology and demographic trends, as there will be no direct contact between your company and the startups.

You'll want to choose your third-party fund carefully, considering only funds whose investment thesis aligns with your corporate strategy. We've frequently seen firms begin their startup investment activity as LPs in a general VC as a way to learn the ropes. As you view the VC's portfolio, you can begin your independent investing by adding additional funding to those startups you view as most promising and befitting for your organization.

The best route for your CVC journey depends on your corporation's goals and the resources at your disposal. Stand-alone CVC funds give you more control and flexibility, but they might take a bit longer to kick off. Direct investments let you move fast, but they come with their own set of risks. Participating in a third-party firm can be a great way to learn, but may not provide the learning you're looking for. In the end, the ideal way to start your CVC adventure hinges on your corporation's unique circumstances. Your chief financial officer (CFO) and board investment committee have a big decision to make!

INVESTMENT THESIS AND GOALS

One of the most important things your CVC needs to function is a clear investment thesis aligned to the firm's overall strategic intent.

As we've said, CVCs always have both strategic and financial goals. After all, if you had no strategic goals and just wanted ROI, there's no particular reason for you to establish your own CVC effort—you might as well keep to your usual business and investment practices. And if you had no financial goals, you might as well stick to other learning engines such as university partnerships or partnership journeys. You're choosing CVC specifically because you want strategy and investment in one package. Each CVC chooses the right balance setting. If you're leaning into strategy, your investment decisions will be tied directly to the firm's needs, while also aiming for financial return. If you're leaning into financial goals, you will need to choose only companies with potential to deliver a huge return, even if their tie to strategy is slight.

Your firm might use a CVC engine for a variety of different strategic goals. For example, Intel Capital invested in order to expand Intel's ecosystem and drive demand for its chips.[11] In addition to ecosystem expansion, other CVC strategic goals include learning about specific technologies, or exploring new business models. In some instances, CVCs have been used to help improve the mergers and acquisitions (M&A) pipeline. Just be aware of potential friction: Your M&A department wants a low price for the companies it purchases, while your CVC arm will be inclined to ask for a high price on the companies it sells.

The investment thesis needs to help potential investees understand what you're looking for so they don't waste time, and help others in the ecosystem understand what you're doing so they can help. The public-facing version doesn't need to articulate your company's quantitative goals. The investment thesis of a CVC arm can follow the same format that VCs use, such as: "[Fund Name] is launching a [$x MM] [Stage] venture fund in [Country/City] to back [Geography] [Sector/Market Companies] [with Secret Sauce]."[12] For example: A CVC focusing on fintech startups in sub-Saharan Africa, looking to back pre-revenue companies, might have a thesis statement along the lines of: *"Four Capital is a $15 MM fund in Nigeria for pre-revenue mobile payment and fintech companies in sub-Saharan Africa leveraging existing mobile infrastructures and partnering with established providers of banking solutions."*

DEVELOP STRONG INFRASTRUCTURE AND OPERATIONS

Once a solid investment thesis is established, it's crucial for the CVC program to align its resources and structure accordingly. The parent company must allocate sufficient resources to support the success of the CVC program. Involve individuals well-versed in VC financing. Without this expertise, corporations may be tempted to approach investments as if they were M&As, asserting control over the emerging company's operations and decision-making. Such an approach can stifle the innovative potential that initially attracted the corporation to invest.

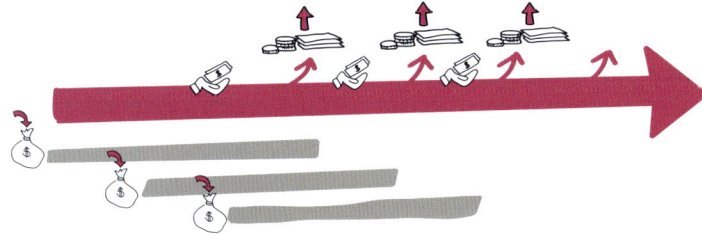

In addition to these considerations, other infrastructure aspects need attention:

Determine the *personnel* who will oversee day-to-day program operations. Whether your CVC is independent or close to the business, leadership should have a mix of VC expertise and corporate strategic insight in order to balance financial returns with long-term innovation goals.

Decision-making structure should be clearly defined—will investment approvals require sign-off from the parent firm's executive board, or will the CVC team have autonomy within predefined limits?

Define the *compensation structure* for the corporate venture team. Traditional VC staff expect incentives tied to the VC fund and its performance—when the fund wins, these incentives can be extremely lucrative, rivaling the salaries of the executives of large firms. That means if you want to attract experienced VC leaders, you may need to do something compelling with your incentives.[13] Consider offering carried interest[14] ("carry" – a performance fee drawn from investment profit) as part of your compensation for fund managers. In CVC, the structure should balance competitive compensation with long-term alignment to the corporation's innovation and strategic goals. Additionally, creating a clear career progression path within the CVC team helps maintain motivation and engagement, ensuring continuity and long-term success

Establish a clear *capital allocation strategy* for the CVC portfolio and targeted investment stages. The parent company needs to decide how much capital will be dedicated annually and whether funding will be distributed in fixed tranches or adjusted based on market conditions and performance. The strategy should also outline the preferred stages of investment—whether the focus will be on early stage startups with high growth potential, later stage companies with proven traction, or a diversified mix across different stages. Defining these parameters ensures that the CVC remains aligned with the company's broader strategic objectives while maintaining financial discipline.

Another part of the CVC's operational landscape is deciding on the investment pattern—will your CVC operate as a *time-limited (closed) fund*, or will it be *evergreen*? Closed fund investment replicates the approach most often taken by general VCs. Specifically, the fund has a certain budget to invest in startups aligned with the thesis over a long period of time (usually ten to twelve years). The fund is allocated at the start. About half of the time is spent sourcing startups and making investments, and the return begins to arrive in the second half. At that point the organization can begin making the case for a second fund. Because the funds are locked and investments are evaluated all at once, there might be a temptation to push startups toward growth or exit before they have achieved their full potential value.

129

Evergreen funds are more flexible—new investments can be made at any time, and new funding can be infused at any time. This frees the CVC to make longer-term decisions. The trade-off is that the success of the overall CVC may be more difficult to measure since each investment operates on a different time frame.

Whether closed or evergreen, investments can be treated individually or as cohorts. Cohort-based investing means the fund decides to invest in a number of startups every year (or any other period of time). Each cohort might be different from the one before it and the one after it—the period allows the CVC to reset intentions and requirements on a regular basis.

The model selected will determine the measurement framework.

TICKET SIZE

The CVC needs to be very clear on the amount they are willing to invest in any given startup (ticket size). Ticket size is tightly tied to the maturity of the startup. The more mature the startup (technology and business model), the lower the risk—and accordingly the higher the value and the more expensive the equity. Conversely, if you invest in early-stage startups with a lower valuation, your money will buy more equity, therefore you can get good value at a smaller ticket size. But the risk of failure is higher. Ticket size can vary dramatically depending on your region, industry, and investment thesis, so customize this decision to your own firm as the CVC is being created. Perhaps it goes without saying: The ticket size you're willing to pay also impacts the number of investments you can make per year given your budget.

PITFALL: Watch out—your investment activity is visible in the ecosystem and has meaningful effects. Your firm's name will appear on your partner's capitalization table (cap table—record of investors), along with the size of your investment. If you're known as a great ecosystem player, your core business complements that of your investee, and your investment is of an appropriate size, your presence can really help your partner. But if other investors think you're going to acquire this company and you don't, or if your investment drives the company's valuation too high for future investment, you can really damage your partner, thereby shooting your own investment in the foot. In practice, this means you probably shouldn't lead investment rounds.

FINANCING YOUR CORPORATE VENTURE CAPITAL

We've seen a variety of different ways to fund your fund. To decide, you'll need to understand your company's environment and align with the key stakeholders.

Consider **internal funding.** The corporation allocates funds from its own resources, such as operating budgets or retained earnings, to finance the CVC. We've even seen one example where the CVC was funded from the risk portion of the firm's retirement fund investment pool. Internal funding provides autonomy and control over investment decisions but requires a long-term, and significant, commitment of capital from the parent company.[15]

challenges. Together, partners pool resources and co-invest in startups. This collaborative approach allows for sharing of financial risk and leveraging of each partner's expertise and networks to identify and support promising investment opportunities. While control is limited, your investment exposure is also limited. Alliance Ventures is a corporate venture capital fund jointly operated by Renault, Nissan, and Mitsubishi, investing in new mobility, autonomous driving, connected services, and EV & energy.[17] The three automotive leaders have carefully determined their participation ratios based on firm requirements, and all three have developed technical collaborations with a subset of portfolio companies. Alliance Ventures is one element in an ecosystem of multiple strategic relationships among these three and other strategic partners.

DELIVERING FUNDS TO YOUR STARTUPS
In the tradition of general VC firms, CVCs frequently use **convertible investment** instruments, such as SAFE (Simple Agreement for Future Equity) notes, which convert into equity if and when any is created through later investment or purchase; or convertible debt notes which can either convert to equity or be repaid at a predetermined time.[18] These instruments allow the startup to raise money before a valuation is established.

When CVCs invest in formal investment rounds, a **traditional** agreement applies: dollars in return for equity. CVCs should very rarely "lead" a round of investment—the leader sets the price, and that's usually an overstrong signal to the market when a corporate body does it. Leave leading to other investors.

Consider your financial resources, strategic objectives, risk tolerance, and the potential benefits and trade-offs associated with each financing option.

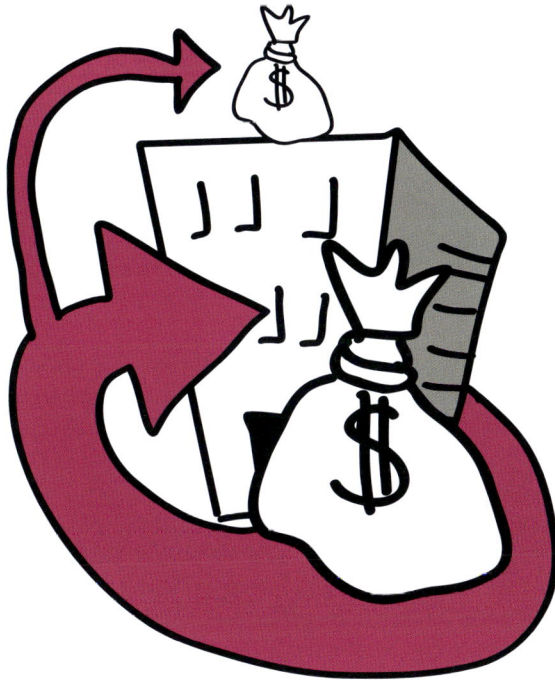

Alternatively, **external funding** is an option. In this setting, the corporation raises capital from outside investors, corporate partners, institutional investors, or sovereign wealth funds interested in participating in the VC space. External funding allows for greater financial flexibility and scalability but requires increased accountability and likely shared ownership or control. Intel Capital, the investment arm of Intel Corporation, spun fully out of the main firm in 2025, at least in part in order to raise capital from external investors to supplement its investment activities.[16]

Strategic partnerships present another approach to funding. In this case, your corporation forms strategic partnerships with other corporations or entities with shared interests or

131

Corporate Venture Capital

Running Your Corporate Venture Capital
ESTABLISH THE DEAL PIPELINE

An important part of any CVC is the deal flow or the deal pipeline, in other words, finding the startups in which to invest. For CVCs, much like for traditional VCs, deal flow is an important activity: The quality of the startups that are being scouted drives the performance of the fund in the long term. Generally speaking, you'll want to consider a very wide range of startups, as few of them will meet your requirements in the long run.

Reach out to startups and entrepreneurs through direct channels, such as cold emails, social media, or industry-specific platforms. These kinds of outreach efforts demonstrate the CVC's interest in potential investment opportunities and encourage entrepreneurs to pitch their businesses to the fund.

In addition, there are many other ways to deal with the issue of deal flow: For example, the CVC can leverage other open innovation engines such as university partnerships, accelerator programs, and business incubators, which all make great sources for potential investment targets.

You can go deeper: Partner with the local startup ecosystem or sponsor large startup events to ensure a significant spotlight on your fund. This kind of activity can be a good basis for PR that shows startups how to find you.

Not to be ignored are investor syndicates. Participating in investor syndicates, or co-investment opportunities with other funds, can provide access to deals that may not be available otherwise. Collaborating with other investors allows for sharing due diligence efforts, outsourcing the task of company valuation, and mitigating risk.

CVCs can also hire third-party vendors to scout for startups more efficiently, in line with the fund's investment thesis and criteria.

By employing a combination of these approaches and remaining proactive, a CVC can ensure a continuous flow of investment opportunities and maintain a competitive edge.

The pipeline is shaped like a funnel. At the very top, you want to be aware of every startup that could possibly be of interest. At full scale, operating like a traditional VC firm, the general lists you'll collect might include a thousand or more companies every year. From there, take meetings with every company that might turn out to meet your needs—perhaps half of the startups on your lists will warrant a conversation. Of those conversations, 10% might make you interested enough to conduct due diligence, a time- and resource-consuming activity. Only invest in those few who make it through that process.[19]

SELECTING YOUR STARTUPS
Invest in startups with a chance to grow their value by orders of magnitude—the risk is significant, but the potential rewards are enormous. This means looking for experienced teams with strong connections (more reliably productive), ideas that are disruptive to a market or represent a technological leap (opportunity for a huge financial win), and existing evidence of market impact (higher chance of success). Financial-leaning CVCs will be attracted to investments that are drawing the attention of lots of other investors—this is "FOMO" (fear of missing out). Strategic-leaning CVCs will seek investments whose activity illuminates an important area of investigation for the firm. Unless you have the experience in-house already, you'll need to bring on or get guidance from an experienced investor who can show you how to draw the right lines for your firm.

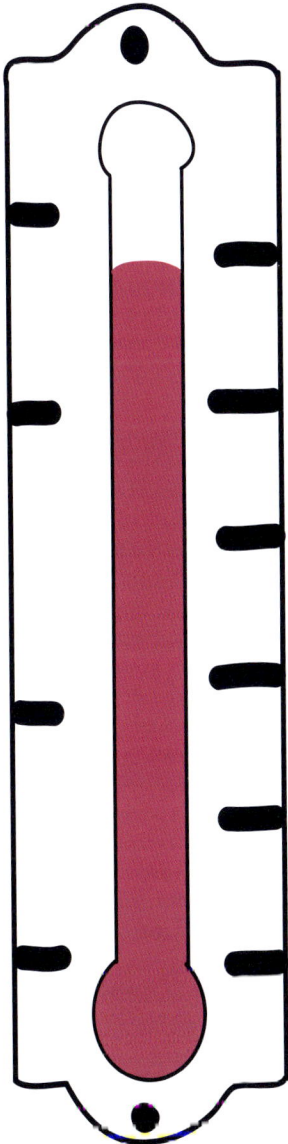

Take care in choosing the startups in which to invest—it's best to have experienced, professional support in selecting your partners. All VCs carefully review their partners—we'll note where CVCs need to approach it differently.

Maturity of technology. Evaluating a startup's technology can start with off-the-shelf frameworks such as the technology readiness level (TRL) commonly used by the National Aeronautics and Space Administration (NASA)[20] and tech companies in general, the manufacturing readiness level (MRL), or others of this type. Tech maturity criteria may be customized somewhat for the needs of your fund—perhaps your risk appetite is high enough to welcome younger, more experimental stages, or perhaps you're in a complex industry where technologies take longer to mature. You will want clear criteria for the maturity of the startups you want to invest in and you'll want to use those criteria throughout your scouting and investment.

Note: The later you invest, the lower the risk, the more expensive the equity, and the less you benefit from the growth (because you already missed much of the growth period).

Business model health. Depending on the maturity level you're going for, you'll test the startup's financial health accordingly. For example, if you're looking at startups that are already in market, you can evaluate market activity—for example, you could require that your startups show a customer lifetime value (CLTV) two times greater than the customer acquisition cost (CAC), or an annual recurring revenue (ARR) of a certain value. If you're investing in earlier startups that do not yet have customers, you can develop confidence in the business model through an expectation that the startup should have already raised capital from other funds. If you're very strategy-oriented and therefore willing to invest in companies with nothing but a strong team and an idea, you can insist that the company be incorporated, insured, and compliant, and leave formal business diligence at that.

Team. The founding team needs to bring experience and perspective you can't get inside your organization. They need to have the technical capacity to execute on the product, service, or platform they're bringing, and the business capacity to take their next step on the journey toward profitability. This nearly always means at least two people with different skill sets. In addition, it is imperative that the team get along well with all relevant stakeholders from your firm. The ideal team is capable of mature discussion even in disagreement, and is coachable when you have guidance.

While experienced founders are more likely to deliver a return, there's a great deal of untapped value in overlooked founders. We strongly recommend making your doors visible so founders you couldn't otherwise find can find you. You'll also want to actively build long-term relationships in the ecosystem for broad visibility into valuable startup activity.

Exit strategy. How does each candidate ultimately aim to return your investment? Are they seeking acquisition, and, if so, by you or someone else? Are they moving toward a public offering? Your due diligence should persuade you that the partner has a credible way to make your equity stake valuable. The founders might change their minds about exit strategy along the way and that could be fine, but to start with you should be clear that there is at least one credible path before you invest.

Market factors. Some of the key considerations here include value proposition (is there a large audience who wants to buy this?) and product differentiation (how are you different from competitors? Is there a "moat" preventing competitors from doing what this startup is doing, but better or cheaper?). Note that private VC is bound by a duty to return a multiple of the fund—orders of magnitude more dollars than originally invested. Therefore, VCs have to be as laser-focused on business success as possible, aiming for potential market leaders in every case. CVCs, given the inclusion of strategic goals, may have a bit more freedom to invest in startups that are compelling for other reasons, such as learning or ecosystem-building, provided they are viable. Viability, that is, likelihood of lasting

as a business at least through the period of your partnership, is a requirement.

Other due diligence. Consider the regulatory environment, talent market, and political climate. Will the startup be able to find the needed staff, get its technology approved or certified as needed, and be accepted by the public?

GROWING YOUR STARTUPS

Your CVC effort is successful to the extent that your startups are successful. So, in addition to your investment, you'll support your startups as best you can, with advice, introductions, market intelligence, etc. As a corporate, you may have special insights, expertise, or other assets that can provide your startups with unique advantages. On the other hand, as a corporate, your advice may be heavily weighted toward your firm's desires, to the detriment of the startup's overall aims. Take care lest you unwittingly harm your own medium/long-term investment by pushing the founders too far toward narrow, short-term outcomes.

Learning from Your Corporate Venture Capital

The CVC engine tends to be less directly learning-oriented and more impact-oriented than some of the others, such as the accelerator or the prove-out journey: On the strategic side you're investing in order to influence your ecosystem or the development trajectory of a technology. On the financial side, you're investing for a return. You can be successful in these activities with very little learning outcome. That said, your close relationship with specific startups can offer a chance to "see around corners,"—in other words, to catch glimpses into and insights from the obstacles and opportunities that your startup partners are nimble enough to encounter and amplify.

If you're eager to exploit the insight power of the CVC, you'll want to make sure that you offer your core business staff frequent and extensive opportunities to work closely with your startups. This of course doubles as an opportunity for the startups to benefit from a close relationship with experts and partners on your staff. This close relationship provides the fastest, most direct way for insights to reach your corporation's front line.

In addition, include learnings in your CVC's reporting. Insights will arrive far faster than actual financial returns. Reporting on your insights can be a great way to show value before any startup delivers an exit. In your dashboarding exercise, did you ensure that the business is set up to receive insights and make changes? If so, that infrastructure will serve well to send insights to the right location for impact. If not, the moment where you realize you want your CVC to be a serious learning channel is a good moment to revisit your learning infrastructure.

"Treat the function as the corporation's science lab and corporate VCs as scientists, always aiming to refute the existing hypotheses, assumptions, and models on which the current business of the corporation is based."

- Gil Press In Forbes Magazine[21]

Measuring this Engine

Measure the right indicators for each stage of the work, and tailor them to your context. In the case of CVC, once well established, you may be preparing, operating, and evaluating the outcomes of certain investments at the same time—it's still helpful to treat these activities as phases, albeit simultaneous phases.

Preparation phase metrics	Operation phase metrics	Outcome phase metrics
• Number of requests for financing (e.g., pitch decks) received per unit of time • Number of companies with which you have had an initial conversation at the top of your funnel—you or they saw enough possibility to bother making a connection • Number of founders you interviewed • Number of companies that sufficiently meet your thesis and investment criteria to justify conducting formal due diligence • Number of investment proposals sent to desirable startups per unit of time • Average fully-burdened cost of attracting one possible investment per unit of time (such as travel, etc.)	• Number of initiated investments per unit of time • Percentage of initiated investments from the total number of companies evaluated • Total invested capital per unit of time • Average ticket size (investment) per unit of time • Average stake taken in ventures per unit of time • Progress of the investment in accordance with a pre-agreed roadmap • Lessons learned per unit of time • Financial impact of lessons learned	• Average cost of taking a stake in a startup including both the Demand phase cost and the Live phase cost per unit of time • New revenue generated per unit of time as a result of investment made • Ratio of new revenue to fully-burdened cost • Business impact (revenue gained or costs reduced) of lessons learned • Portfolio value appreciation per unit of time • Portfolio value appreciation to cost ratio (total cost of venturing including the internal costs such as salaries of the responsible people) per unit of time • Ratio of all value (learning, increased equity value) to fully burdened costs • Collaboration-specific outcomes mutually agreed upon at the start of each collaboration (may vary from venture to venture)

Sunsetting Corporate Venture Capital

When the time comes, at the planned end of your closed fund or when your analysis of your evergreen fund drives toward closure, sunsetting a CVC program requires an approach that ensures both smooth transition and minimal disruption to ongoing operations and investments.

Developing a closure strategy is integral to the sunsetting process. This strategy should detail how to depart from current investments, whether through selling stakes, transferring ownership, or winding down operations, in a way that maximizes value and minimizes losses. It's also important to determine if any strategic partnerships or collaborations with portfolio companies can continue outside the CVC framework (maybe via other open innovation vehicles). A well-planned closure strategy protects the company's interests and preserves valuable relationships.

Financial and legal considerations are a central component of sunsetting a CVC. Conduct a comprehensive review of all legal agreements and obligations to avoid any unforeseen liabilities. Financial planning should address outstanding commitments and potential financial impacts, ensuring the company is prepared for any financial implications of the closure. Reallocate human and financial resources to integrate the changes smoothly into the company's broader strategy.

Finally, document the learnings and outcomes from the CVC program. Review the program's successes and challenges, and preserve key insights that can inform future strategic decisions. Ensuring that knowledge and relationships built through the CVC program are transferred to relevant teams within the organization to maintain continuity.

Announce the closure publicly. Meet all regulatory and reporting requirements for a formal and compliant end to the program. By following these steps, a company can effectively sunset its CVC program, mitigating risks and preserving value for the organization.

8

CHAPTER EIGHT

Prove-out Journey

For this engine, think of the scale scores as a starting point. As each journey unfolds, you'll have many decision opportunities where you can increase visibility, adjust your demand for speed, or up the financial stakes.

Prove-out journey is our name for chains of joint projects between your firm and another entity. The prove-out journey is a planned series of engagements that increase in their depth and value over time, provided results point in that direction. Such a journey might begin with a mutual nondisclosure agreement (NDA), and move on to a Simple Partnership Agreement (SiPA) and/or materials transfer agreement (MTA), followed by a proof of concept (POC), a venture client agreement, a joint research agreement (JRA), a joint venture (JV), or even an acquisition. All the acronyms might make this process sound like random alphabet soup. It's more powerful to recognize that these familiar acronyms signal grounding in familiar project-types that have already withstood the tests of time. By chaining them together in a single journey with a single partner (at a time), you convert them from a general library of standard processes to an effective open innovation engine. A prove-out journey can be a compelling way to access the agility, knowledge, and risk appetite of other organizations. While we'll be discussing these journeys in the context of startup engagement, you can take a similar journey with peer organizations or others in your ecosystem. We've even seen these journeys work with consultants!

The biggest difference between the prove-out journey (when done well) and the other engines is that each individual partnership is owned by the core business. You'll only initiate partnerships that a business unit already desires. The internal partner is always someone who needs the result for their own decision-making, research, or profit and loss (P&L) within the large organization. As a result, there's no formal upper or lower limit on the number of partnerships and journeys your organization can undertake. You can try one anytime, you can have as many as make sense for your particular organization, and you can start one or stop one at any time according to the needs of your stakeholders. When it comes to prove-out journeys, the job of your open innovation engine team is more about identifying internal needs and scouting external solutions than it is about managing the engine itself.

Speed to Results

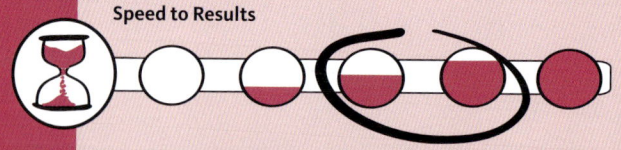

Potential Size of Financial Impact

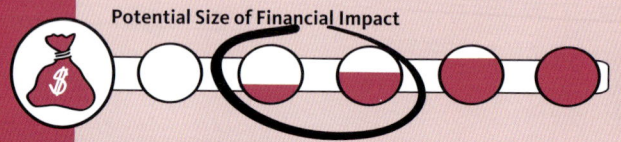

Scope of Cultural Impact

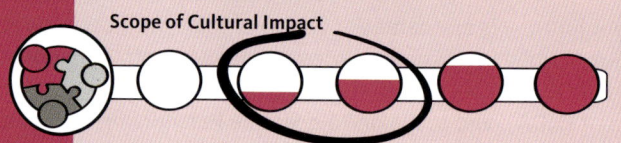

Visibility

Learning Opportunity

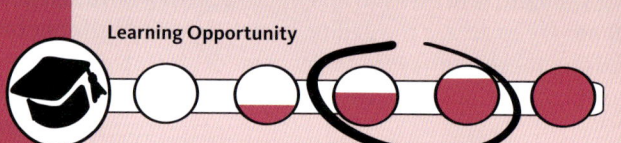

Degree of Corporate Control

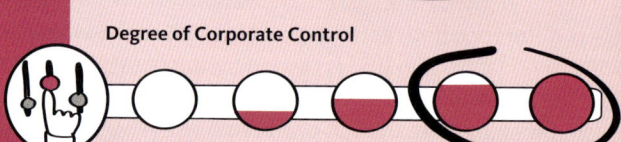

Resources Required

Demand for Speed

Potential Size of Financial Impact

Scope of Cultural Impact

Visibility

Learning Opportunity

Degree of Corporate Control

Resources Required

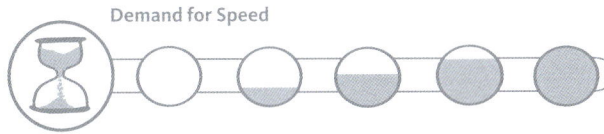

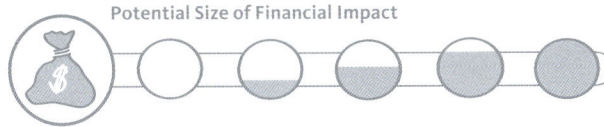

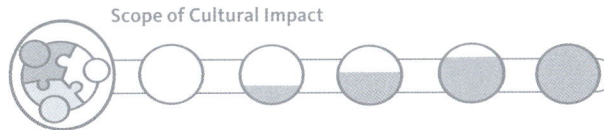

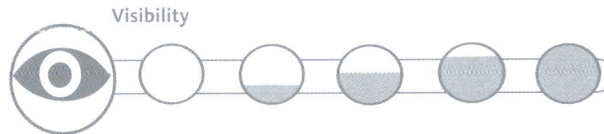

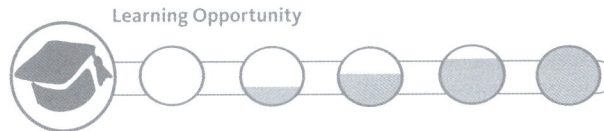

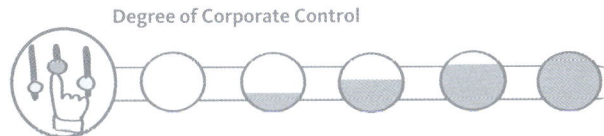

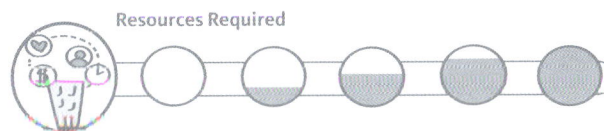

Bend the
back cover flap
over this page
to see your scales
and the Engine's scales
side by side.

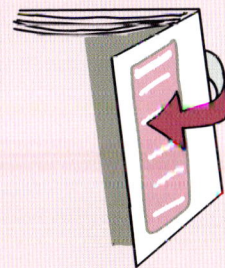

Prove-out Journey Scales

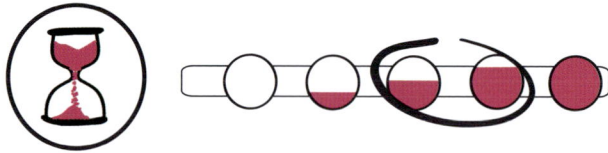

SPEED TO RESULTS:
Full alignment to drive revenue.

Your partner wants to engage with you specifically because you are large and represent a solid, significant, potentially company-changing level of revenue as well as a source of game-changing information and in-kind resources. You're going forward with them because they carry the right maturity level and interests/needs to address your next question on the path to revenue. In other words, you're fully on the same page about aiming to make money. Given these shared goals, you're bound to move toward revenue fairly rapidly. Perhaps you'll be ready to make money together soon, or perhaps you'll speedily rule out an important dead end so you don't waste money.

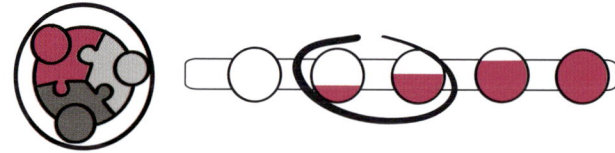

POTENTIAL SIZE OF FINANCIAL IMPACT:
Each partnership has at least a small shot.

In a prove-out journey, you're engaging specifically to explore financial impact down the line.

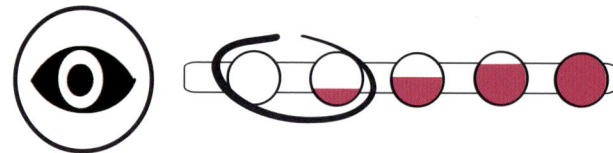

SCOPE OF CULTURAL IMPACT:
The practice of prove-out journeys can have broad impact, if done right.

Prove-out journeys are driven by internal staff. To make them happen, you'll open an innovation door that your internal leaders might not have noticed before. Your internal communications about the opportunity can have meaningful cultural impact. Those internal staff who choose to engage get extensive exposure to the partner and their way of approaching work. Real inspiration and shifts can happen in this context. How far this cultural impact goes depends on the way staff ultimately get involved in journeys.

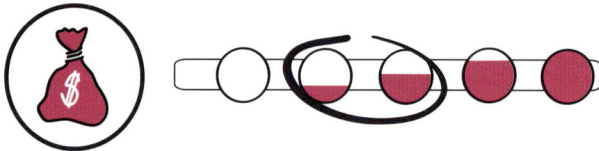

VISIBILITY:
Each journey gets its own visibility setting.

One charm of a prove-out journey approach is that its visibility is fully adjustable. You can shout a partnership from the rooftops if it's in line with your communication goals. If there's no particular value in stakeholder awareness, simply report each partnership where required (e.g., in your quarterly financials). Similarly, you can publicize the journey engine as a program, or simply quietly work through individual partnerships.

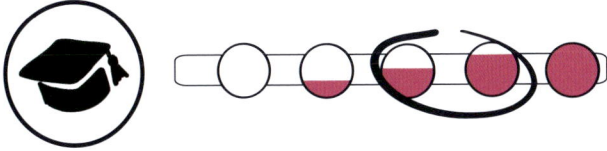

LEARNING OPPORTUNITY:
Every prove-out journey will generate learning.

You're choosing partners to address specific knowledge gaps for specific internal leaders. Revenue is intended, and learning is guaranteed, whether or not the revenue eventually arrives. Any learning generated will be limited to the internal group sponsoring the partnership, unless you design to extend the learning more broadly.

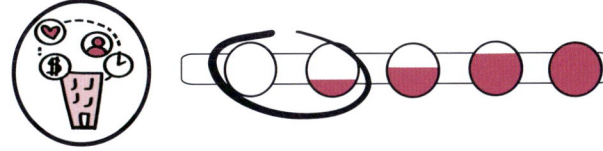

RESOURCES REQUIRED: BETWEEN 1 AND 2 (AND MAY GROW)
Prove-out journeys start cheap and grow to reasonable, de-risking along the way.

Staff inside the large organization must participate directly in order for a prove-out journey to work. While the dollars involved may not be very high, especially at the start of the journey, the hours involved may be significant. Staff time must be absolutely committed in order for this to work.

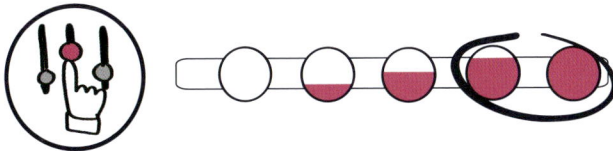

DEGREE OF CORPORATE CONTROL:
Your influence and power over the partner are significant—wield them wisely.

The Intimacy of a partnership on a prove-out journey means that internal staff with material expertise are in the room with the startup, and the intentions of the collaboration are defined up front on paper. As the corporate, you engage when and how you wish, and you can make or break the project. Given this power, it's important to ensure that you're operating in a founder-friendly fashion—protect your partner's secrets, share wins as well as losses, deliver obligations in a timely fashion, be transparent.

143

Prove-out Journey

Why You Should Choose This Engine

Prove-out journey partnerships allow for maximum flexibility—engage when, and only when, needs and opportunities align. Obligations are limited to each individual project with a signed contract; otherwise, you haven't promised anything to anyone. That's a significant contrast with other engagement engines where you're announcing a commitment. Your partners strongly prefer these intimate journeys where they work alongside internal business staff and receive real feedback from their eventual specific customer or partner. When your partner is a startup, that real-world feedback is far more valuable to them than pro bono advice from a generic mentor. Your goals will be strongly aligned, and neither party wastes time.

Why You Shouldn't Choose This Engine

Don't engage in prove-out journey partnerships if you're not ready. Bad agreements or journeys can be toxic to your reputation in the ecosystem, so you'll need to start with some key basics for healthy partnerships: A fast track to payment for your partners (if paying), accountable time from the internal leaders, and careful limits on reporting or other paperwork demands from your partners. If you can't make those things happen, prove-out journeys aren't right for your organization.

Making Prove-out Journeys Work

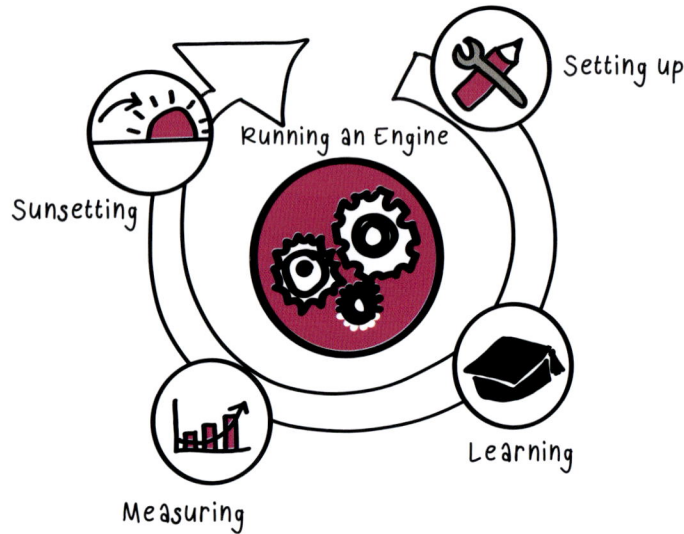

Running an Engine

Setting up

Sunsetting

Learning

Measuring

You've chosen to move forward with the partnership engine that carries the deepest connection between partners: the prove-out journey. Your goal in this kind of partnership engine is to test and prove (or fail) a hypothesis (or more than one), and if all goes well, to move forward together to a deeper step. Many firms take such journeys on an ad hoc basis—sometimes the right way to work outside the building is to simply dance with one partner at a time. We advocate for something a bit more systematic, where partnerships are tracked and the resulting technologies and lessons learned are adopted. If you're providing structured support for executing and learning from prove-out journey partnerships, and tracking them consistently, you've got an engine. In this handbook, we're leaning into our strength in corporate–startup partnership— similar principles apply to exploring with a peer, government agency, not-for-profit, or other partner.

To start, some things partners can do together:

Concept validation test: Nontechnical exploration of the value of creating a given product or service, before the product or service is created. Uses props, stories, and/or images to gather customer or user feedback on the idea. Answers questions such as: How much do people care about this problem? Would this solution solve it for them? What resistance or hungers might change how we move forward with the product or service? Also known as a low-fidelity prototype test.

Medium- or high-fidelity prototype test: Evaluation of a working or near-working prototype to gather feedback on its use. Answers questions such as: Is the interface simple enough to use? How can we make the product or service more convenient or appealing?

Proof-of-concept (POC): Here you're agreeing to test whether a hope or hypothetical can be made real by the two partners working together. Does the proposed technology or service really work as intended or advertised? The POC is a technical demonstration that a concept will function as a product (or service) in your circumstances. Answers questions such as: If we add our ingredient to our partner's ingredient, will the resulting material actually turn out to be stronger? Or: If we run our unique question through our partner's software, will we get a useful result?

Pilot: A pilot differs from a POC in that it is a market test— what happens when we attempt to sell or use the solution in the field? A pilot is the first in-market test of a working product. Address market questions such as: What are the obstacles to purchase? What are the usage patterns? What can we do to encourage widespread adoption?

In a prove-out journey, you and your partner walk through some of these tests together on your way to a possible outcome. The prove-out journey serves as an element of due diligence, allowing the two organizations to get to know each other and the technical and business realities. The journey can take you to a variety of different ends:

Investment: Your firm provides cash and other considerations in exchange for equity.

Joint research agreement (JRA) or Joint development agreement (JDA): You and your partner work together to complete an investigation or a product/service. You each contribute to the work, and you each benefit.

Joint venture: You create a new, separate business together with shared ownership. This is often temporary on the way to a further outcome.

Licensing or purchase: Renting or buying a patent, product, or other complete asset. In licensing, your partner owns an invention and you pay them to use it—in a purchase you buy the invention outright. If you act as one of the partner's first paying customers for a finished product or service, and allow them to tell the world about it, your license or purchase is *venture clienting*—we'll say more about that in the final chapter.

Acquisition: Buying the partner's company, in whole or in part. In other words, in this setting your prove-out journey engine serves to support your mergers and acquisitions (M&A) activity—the prove-out journey is a type of deep, field-based, relationship-building due diligence.

Setting Up Your Prove-out Journey Engine
PERSONNEL

Engine team: In a prove-out journey partnership engine, the primary job of the engine team is to foster, support, and track relationships between the core business and external partners. Therefore, you need the right number of people to manage the number of journeys you want. If you're not already doing this, you might start with just a single journey, in which case a fraction of time from a program manager will do to start.

Internal partners (core business): Ideally, each journey is set up so that a core business person has something at stake: They really care about the results at each stage of the journey and therefore they're the person who works the hardest on that journey. The engine team (see previous paragraph) simply facilitates. The internal partner is a specific person in the core business who acts as the external partner's counterpart. Depending on the project, this might be a scientist, engineer, product leader, or business owner. This person understands and feels responsible for the question or challenge under investigation with the external partner. They drive the project forward to address their own professional motives, and they are responsible for following intellectual property (IP) guidelines and nondisclosure. In your engine, you'll also ask them to be responsible for some (minimal, infrequent, and high-value) progress reporting. That's the only demand that the engine team gets to make—otherwise the internal partner is there to pursue business goals based on their own instincts, expertise, and interest.

We have frequently seen large organizations run POCs, or even pilots, from the engine team alone, with the hope that the core business will gladly receive the results once achieved and the journey can be handed off. From experience, we strongly recommend involving the core business from the beginning. Taking on new research, products, or services entails enormous trade-offs for the core business—shifting resources away from a cash cow, altering processes, retooling machines, etc. You're much more likely to see adoption of the results of a POC or pilot if the core business cares enough to invest labor from the very beginning. That way, the POC or pilot team can understand and prepare for any obstacles to adoption, and the business line team can anticipate and plan for any necessary changes. In an ideal world, each internal partner for a journey is aligned to your Open Innovation Dashboard (see The Open Innovation Dashboard chapter in the first half of the book).

INTELLECTUAL PROPERTY
We recommend keeping intellectual property (IP) simple: Background IP, that is, IP created by either party before the partnership journey begins, belongs to that party going forward. Foreground IP, that is, IP created through the partnership, belongs to both parties. You can decide that the parties must make decisions about foreground IP together, or that each party can separately use the foreground IP as desired without consulting the other party. You can have even (50/50) or uneven ownership of the foreground IP, provided the parties agree up front.

AGREEMENTS AND ARRANGEMENTS
Your prove-out journey partnerships must be grounded in clear, written, mutual understanding at every step along the way. Let's go through the alphabet soup of documents that mark the milestones along a prove-out partnership journey, in rough journey order.

NONDISCLOSURE AGREEMENT
A nondisclosure agreement (NDA) that protects a partner is quite a serious matter for a corporate—often startups don't realize this. We've seen novice founders ask corporates to sign an NDA before the first conversation, before they even tell

you their wonderful idea. That's not appropriate and you must decline for several reasons. First, if the founder can't safely say what problem they're solving or anything at all about their general approach, it's probably a perpetual motion machine or other fantasy, and it's not a good use of your time to listen.

Second, ideas happen when the time is right, and that's when all of the underlying technology and science are present to make the idea possible to conceive. And at that moment, multiple people think of the idea at the same time. When Alexander Graham Bell invented the telephone, he literally raced to the patent office to get there before a competitor. Since every emerging idea is ready to emerge through multiple sources, there may not be much value to your partner in keeping so much of their idea a secret.

Third, an NDA is a real undertaking for your firm. Like any agreement, it represents mitigation, as well as preparation for a future lawsuit. What if you sign an NDA and it turns out someone else in the firm had the same idea as your startup already? Unlucky timing could cause the appearance of a disclosure violation. A thorough internal review to prevent and track disclosure takes time.

Investors, such as venture capitalists (VCs), often decline to sign any NDAs whatsoever for these reasons.[1]

The founder needs to find a way to explain enough to encourage a second conversation, without requiring an NDA. Asking for an NDA before any conversation at all is a sign of an immature founder who lacks confidence in their own IP strategy and would make a difficult partner. If the founder insists, walk away, you're saving yourself a lot of trouble.

What about from your side? Make sure you're on the same page with your legal team—they may have a position about when you should ask your startup partner to sign an NDA. It's founder-friendly to find a way to talk about your interests prior to asking your partner to sign an NDA that protects you, especially since you likely won't sign one that protects them right away.

Ultimately, you will likely need to sign an NDA that protects both you and your partner when it's time to get into the technical nitty-gritty of the project. Care for your partner's IP, and an expectation of their respect for yours, are partnership requirements.

149

With that in mind, before you take the first step in your first prove-out journey, you'll want to confirm with your legal department who in the firm is qualified to sign, and, if possible, negotiate with them to permit a single signature, from someone as low as possible in the organization chart.

Review your firm's existing NDA template. Quite often these have been designed to protect you in arrangements with large peer organizations who bring armies of lawyers. Your NDA may be complex and many pages long. When you partner with a startup to explore a concept, they might not have access to even a single lawyer, nor the time to review. You need a simpler format in this setting. You can offer to use your partner's mutual NDA template, or you can work with your own legal department up front to create a special NDA for this setting—aim for one to two pages with clear and simple language. Work in the spirit of our commandments for founder friendliness: Communicate, and respect your partner's time. For speed and reputation, prepare before your first partnership with a simple NDA you can sign, or prebook time from a department attorney who can evaluate and sign your partner's NDA.

If your legal department will approve, often the easiest way to move forward is to use the founder's NDA.

MEMORANDUM OF UNDERSTANDING

To begin outlining the partnership, use a memorandum of understanding (MOU) as the vehicle to negotiate elements and come to clarity. While not technically binding, you'll use the MOU to convey each party's clearest intentions on all points of negotiation. The attorneys can take it from there. (Do make sure you know what your legal department will generally agree to before you begin and stay within their lines as you develop the MOU—it's terribly disappointing when a frontline innovation person gets a founder excited about a possibility that the corporate legal department later forbids.) For firms with high innovation maturity and for small projects, provided the internal team is genuinely able to deliver the funds and other elements of the understanding, an MOU may be sufficient—you'll want to check this with your legal department first!

SIMPLE PARTNERSHIP AGREEMENT

We've seen over and over again that a weighty contract shuts down good partnerships. They simply take too long, and are too expensive for founders to review. The non-profit organization, Activate, made the same observation and decided to do something about it. In partnership with DLA Piper, and with communication support from Diana Joseph, they created and freely shared the Simple Partnership Agreement (SiPA)[2]—an industry-tested, two-page agreement designed to suit either a procurement process or a contract process, as needed. Deliverables and dates are attached to the agreement as an Exhibit A. We strongly recommend asking your legal department to review and approve it as a template, before you initiate your first partnership.

MATERIALS TRANSFER AGREEMENT

In order to test your partner's product, you might need them to send it to you, in which case you'll need a materials transfer agreement (MTA). To be founder-friendly, you should pay to cover your partner's time and materials, and you'll need to confirm recognition of the partner's background IP (see earlier section, "Intellectual Property"). Even better: Share data from your test of the material, even, and especially, if you choose not to use it. The US National Institutes of Health provides a standard agreement format you can use or modify.[3]

INVESTMENT AGREEMENT

At some point along the journey, you might choose to invest in your partner's company, both to provide them with some cash, and to access a return for yourself. This can be a great way to

align intentions—now you're both committed to the partner's growth. It's terribly important to keep this investment bounded, even though both you and your partner might be tempted to consider a large investment. Here's why: A big investment can ruin your partner's capitalization (cap) table (public-facing investment record). Either you're taking a great deal of equity to match your big investment, in which case other investors might be concerned about your degree of control; or you're "generously" taking not too much equity, in which case your partner's valuation skyrockets. It can be exciting for founders to have a high valuation, but it makes it much harder for them to raise a higher round in the future. Either way, you could be closing the door to future investment for that partner. Talk this through carefully with your partner and act when you find the sweet spot—an investment of just the right size to send healthy signals to the market.

JOINT DEVELOPMENT AGREEMENT / JOINT RESEARCH AGREEMENT

A joint development agreement (JDA) lays out expectations: Who will license what prior inventions to whom? Who will bear which costs? What are the deadlines? A joint research agreement (JRA) can be considered a subtype of a JDA. It's crucial to establish which party owns which rights to discoveries uncovered together. Importantly, having a written joint agreement in place means that, at least in the US, the US Patent Office will consider revelations made during the agreed-upon work as an exception to prior art. In other words, a combined team with a JDA (or JRA) can talk to each other freely about the invention without damaging their chances of receiving a patent.[4]

A prove-out journey is an intimate setting, with your staff and startup staff working closely together on a project. They are both bound to learn something that influences their work in the future, regardless of how bullet-proof your NDA language is. Ensure everyone understands this and is prepared for the consequences. What will happen if one of your engineers catches an insight that ultimately changes your firm's development path to the detriment of your partner? A JDA is a good way to reassure both parties that their interests remain aligned.

FINDING AND SELECTING YOUR PARTNERS

Outbound: You might have needs for which you're seeking partners—in this case you will operate something like a scouting team. In fact, you might simply add innovation-level requests to your scouting list, inviting your scouts to bring earlier partners that might not be ready for the M&A or licensing you were already doing. You can also publicly announce your intention to partner, either generally speaking or in regards to specific questions or challenges you're pursuing.

Inbound: Potential partners, such as startups and peers, may have their own ideas about initiating a journey with you. If you're open to this, make yourself available—announce which conferences you're attending, put up a "partner with us" page on your website with a contact form and/or email address, share your professional social media tags when you speak, and be sure to read messages you receive there.

There's no cohort with a prove-out journey engine, and no external limit on the number of partnerships appropriate for your firm. The right number comes simply from your firm's strategic intent and internal limitations.

NEGOTIATIONS

In a prove-out journey with a startup, you are the Goliath—take care you don't crush David, and also watch for stones flying at your head. You can take advantage of the uneven circumstances to create win-win scenarios:

- Expect to pay for time and materials—an appropriate and meaningful amount for the startup will be a rounding error on a rounding error for your firm. You get what you asked for and a generous helping of good will for almost nothing.

- Expect to share the effort. Your in-kind contributions can make a huge difference. Consider marketing or legal support, and access to your customers or suppliers, research space, datasets, or equipment.
- Expect to share the benefits. You and your partner both need to receive benefits—what's the appropriate split? 50-50? Or is their contribution deserving of a higher proportion? Or, given that the power of each dollar is higher for them, should they be satisfied with a lower proportion of a huge win?

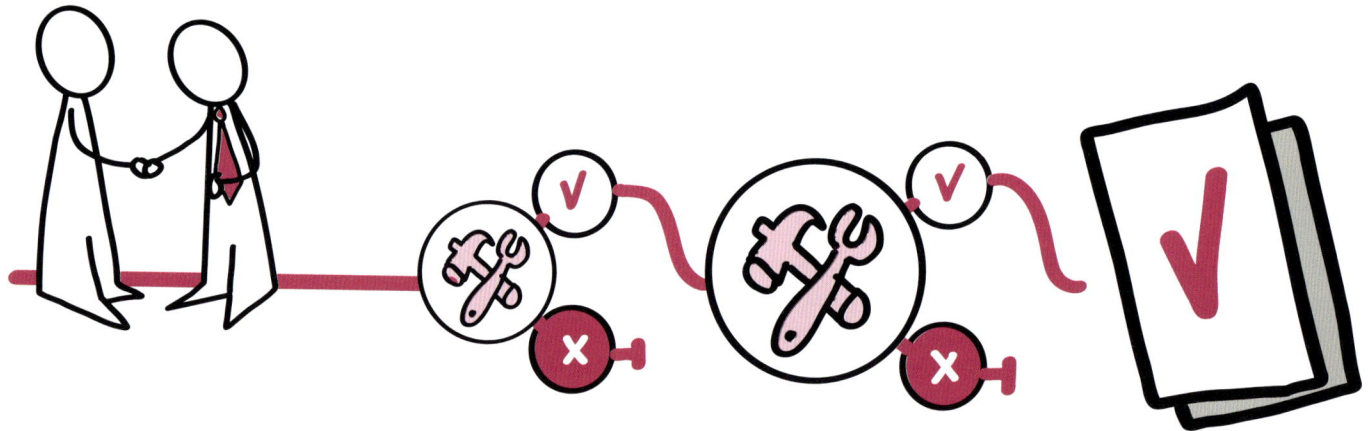

Running Each Prove-out Journey

Each journey begins by finding a suitable partner who can solve a known problem for the business (or perhaps reveals a previously unrecognized problem worth solving). Together, the partners identify the right first research question to address, and the right project type to address it. They create an appropriate agreement and sally forth. When the findings arrive, it's time to consider next steps—will we study another question through another project, close the partnership, or take some more substantial next step together?

The engine team's responsibilities focus on identifying the challenge, scouting the partner, bringing in the legal resources in a smooth fashion, and making sure a result is delivered and documented. The business owner may work much more closely with the partner, or delegate the partner to uncover the answers.

Prove-out journeys have built-in closure gates. At the end of each phase of the journey, follow the results. Do they indicate you should take another step? Change the possible outcome intentions? Or stop here? When you choose to end, a friendly farewell is in order to maintain optionality on helping each other in the future. Provide feedback, listen thoughtfully to your partner's feedback, and move on.

SUPPORTING THE INTERNAL PARTNER

The internal partner is a core business stakeholder. You want them focused on business outcomes from their prove-out journey. You can scaffold them for noncore matters such as agreements, administration, and the partner search. Identify partners for them. Provide them with a curated library of preapproved agreement language, easy access to the legal department (monthly or quarterly office hours?), a simple way to be on the radar of the M&A team in case things move in that direction. Tell them what you need to track from a metrics point of view, and how often. If possible, offer to have the engine team conduct the tracking. Check in regularly and provide guidance as to next steps. Look for ways to make their partnership work easier. Look for ways to make them look good with leadership. Train them on appropriate time and technical information boundaries, and on when to say no.

Learning from Prove-out Journeys

Because the internal business partner is engaged from the beginning, learnings go directly into the business. That's great, but you can miss the chance to spread the benefits more broadly. The innovation engine team should take responsibility for documenting insights and business impact, and making them available to others in the organization, for example, the diverse open innovation squad/advisory board who built your Open Innovation Dashboard in the first place.

Measuring Prove-out Journeys

As with all engines, measure the right indicators for each phase of your work, and customize them from our suggested foundation to your context. Customization is especially important in the prove-out journey engine where each journey could be very different from others.

Preparation phase metrics	Operation phase metrics	Outcome phase metrics
• Number of reach-out messages received from startups interested in a prove-out journey with your company, in a unit of time • Percentage of startups accepted in a prove-out journey from the number of startups considered	• Percentage of challenge owners (internal business stake-holders) who are successfully matched with at least one appropriate partner • Average time spent in the first "leg" (initial project) of the journey • Average time required to "kill" a partnership (e.g., by demonstrating that the initial hypothesis was a dead end) • Average conversion rate from one prove-out journey stage to the next • Prove-out journey and business model-specific metrics demonstrating progress and/or potential to achieve the desired outcomes • Satisfaction scores (e.g., net promoter score (NPS) from external partners in the prove-out journey • Satisfaction scores from internal employees and/or stake-holders regarding the prove-out journey program(s)	• Prove-out journey-spe-cific impact metrics (e.g., ROI, social impact, reve-nue, CLTV etc.) • Number of documented insights generated in unit of time (can be measured both while the prove-out journey is in full swing and as a cumulative num-ber across journeys at an appropriate cadence (e.g., annually). • Overall end-to-end suc-cess rate (e.g., converting partnering startup to supplier if that was the purpose of the prove-out journey, producing pat-ents or papers, generat-ing revenue)

Sunsetting Your Prove-out Journey Engine

Don't want to do prove-out journeys anymore? Just stop doing them! It's that simple. Finish the agreements you have and don't start another. Assign innovation staff to other open innovation responsibilities. Remember to inform any internal staff who might have been looking forward to the next one, and take down any posted form or email you were using to collect inbound interest. All of that said: Why don't you want to do prove-out journeys anymore? They're low-effort, high-value ways of learning and generating tangible impact from the outside world.

9

CHAPTER NINE

University
Partnership

The power of open innovation comes from the difference between your motives and strengths and those of your partners. Nowhere is that more salient than in the context of university partnership. You are a commercial entity driven by commerce in the present, challenged to understand how the world will change and how to sell into that world. Universities are driven to investigate the bleeding edge, explore frontier science, develop novel insights and grow investigators.[1] But they lack the capacity to bring their science, technology, insights, and investigators into the real world on their own. Working together, you get access to the future, and the university gets to see their research come to real-world fruition.

Let's talk about university partnership *as an open innovation practice*. (Large organizations famously appear in campus settings, for example, in named buildings and sports arenas. You don't need this book for that.) The obvious reason to invest in university partnership is to **stay ahead of groundbreaking research.** You want eyes in the laboratories of the investigators whose findings are likely to change your field, so that you're aware of insights and can enhance or mitigate their effects as early as possible. There's another important benefit to working with universities: **Access to the innovation talent pipeline**. Through partnership, you'll have an opportunity to work side by side with faculty, graduate students, and postdoctoral fellows who might very much like to come work for your organization at the next stage of their career. Or perhaps the researchers will become startup founders who can de-risk concepts that ultimately benefit you. In addition to developing scientific and engineering minds, academia is a deeply entrepreneurial field. Faculty, graduate students, and postdoctoral fellows are strongly incentivized to be independent thinkers, so bringing them into, or alongside, your organization can be a source of entrepreneurial thinking.

157

University Partnership

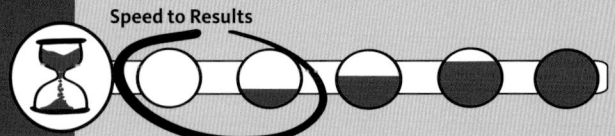

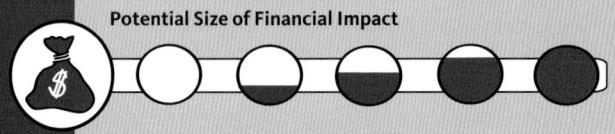

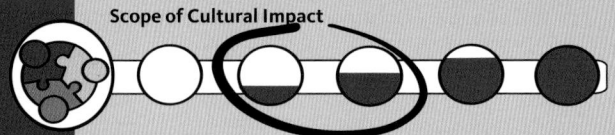

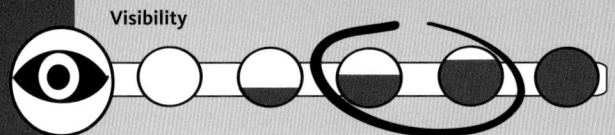

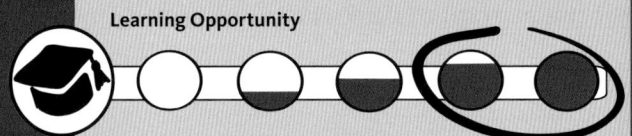

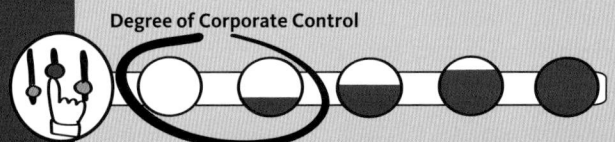

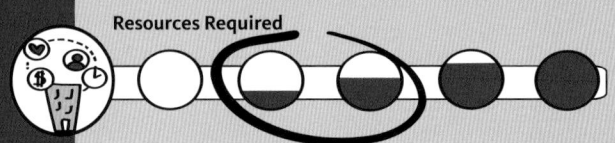

Speed to Results

Potential Size of Financial Impact

Scope of Cultural Impact

Visibility

Learning Opportunity

Degree of Corporate Control

Resources Required

?

Demand for Speed

Potential Size of Financial Impact

Scope of Cultural Impact

Visibility

Learning Opportunity

Degree of Corporate Control

Resources Required

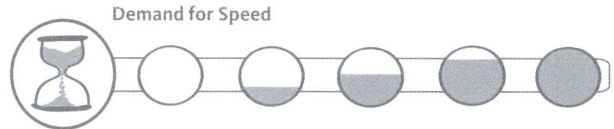

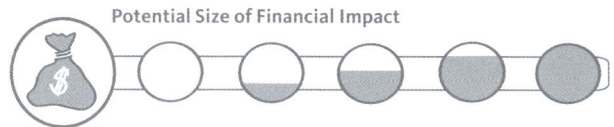

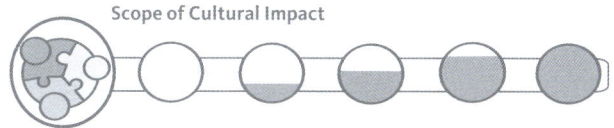

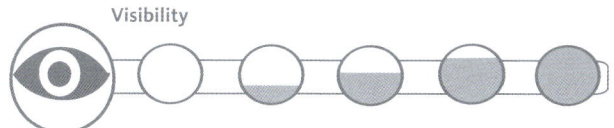

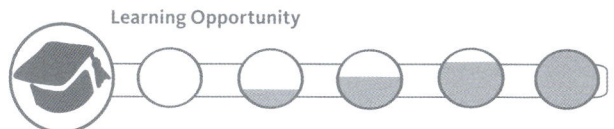

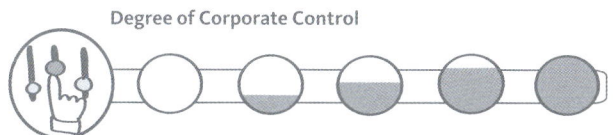

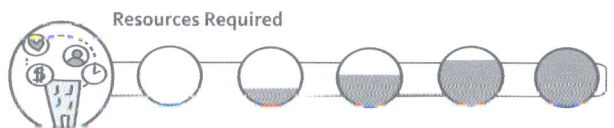

Bend the
back cover flap
over this page
to see your scales
and the Engine's scales
side by side.

University Partnership Scales

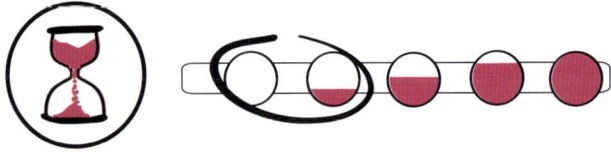

SPEED TO RESULTS:
Financial results will take a long time (other results can be pretty fast!).

University sponsorship is a long-term play—your purpose is to get in on the ground floor of ideas that are completely new. Depending on the field of endeavor, you may wait many years, or even decades, before an idea hatched in the laboratory will be ripe for commercialization. So, we've set this scale at the highest level of patience required. That said: Access to talent begins much sooner, within a year or two. And there's always the possibility of inspiration flow between the university and the corporate—that can start right away.

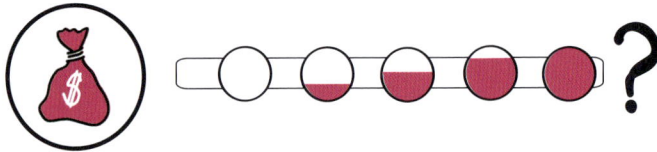

POTENTIAL SIZE OF FINANCIAL IMPACT:
Financial impact is difficult to attribute.

Chances are you will find it difficult to compute the financial impact of a university partnership. For example, do you attribute all of the profits and expenses associated with a new hire from the university to the partnership? Or some portion of those profits and expenses? What portion? If university research plays a role in some commercial activity in five or ten years, what portion of that activity will be attributable to the university, and how will you manage the reconciliation be-

tween activities in the present and a decade in the past? Once the activity happens, you may be able to execute a plausible calculation, and the impact may be significant. Our recommendation is to come to the question of financial impact without preconceived notions. Given this context, university partnership best serves large organizations when they treat it as a general power source, rather than a product line.

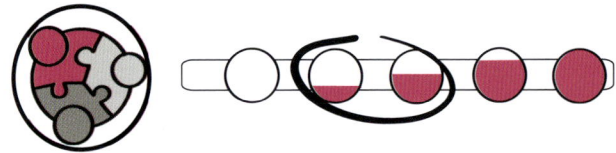

SCOPE OF CULTURAL IMPACT:
Design carefully if you want cultural impact.

Typically, university activities are located on the university campus, not on the large organization campus. As such, it's very difficult for organization staff to participate in university activities with any depth. That said, we've seen large energy companies and large chemical companies make a serious attempt by placing staff on campus at the university as part of the partnership. These "bridgers" report to the organization but spend every day at the university. Their responsibility is to gather scientific, ecosystem, and hiring pipeline insights. *If the large organization is well set up to receive those insights*, there's an opportunity for cultural impact. Over the very long run, as university talent comes into the large organization or develops startups that partner with the large organization, those voices can also move the organization in a more entrepreneurial direction.

VISIBILITY:
Decide with your partner how much energy to put into visibility.

Visibility for university partnership is somewhere in the middle range. They are a good way to let your audience know that you're interested in the future and in young scholars. As they are pretty standard, announcing a university partnership probably won't by itself put you on any new maps. You'll be going forward with your partner, so you can align your visibility goals and go forth together.

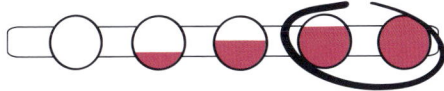

LEARNING OPPORTUNITY:
The very point!
The primary purpose of the university partnership is learning. By investing in frontline investigation activity, you are bound to learn something about the science, technology, or behavior your university partners are investigating. And through that activity, you're bound to learn about your partners and their staff and students. Note though—you can miss this opportunity if you're not prepared to receive it.

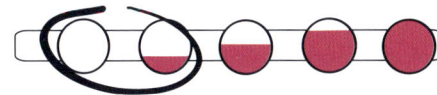

DEGREE OF CORPORATE CONTROL:
Refrain from overcontrol.

The degree of corporate control should be thought of as low, though somewhat tuneable for university partnerships—you'll agree to a plan before the work begins, and you can decide: Are you simply funding the work that a professor's lab is already doing, in return for insights? Or are you influencing a research group down a path you have in mind? Use caution when asserting control from the large organization's side: Whenever you establish guardrails on investigator activities, you're closing intellectual doors for business reasons. You'll certainly frustrate your partner—worse, you might miss something important and never know it.

RESOURCES REQUIRED:
Kind to the open innovation wallet.

Generally speaking, researchers very much appreciate funding and can get a great deal done for fairly low investment. (Naming rights for a building or stadium might be a completely different story—that sort of sponsorship is outside of our swim lane!)

161

University Partnership

Why You Should Choose This Engine

University partnership is almost entirely free of risk. The price can be low relative to other partnership engines, you're certain to meet people who might be great future employees or partners, and you get an opportunity to view science at the cutting edge. The lessons you learn can be applied immediately to your investigation and investment strategies. If you want high visibility, university sponsorship activity is potentially newsworthy. And if you don't want high visibility, you simply refrain from advertising and PR (naturally you'll still include it in required reporting). If you're just dipping a toe into open innovation, and you don't have to prove return on investment (ROI) anytime soon, sponsoring university research can be a great place to start.

Why You Shouldn't Choose This Engine

University research by definition unfolds at the lab stage, or even the whiteboard stage, well below the technology readiness level you'll need to commercialize what you learn. In-market products based on university research may be years or even decades away. Some universities have sophisticated technology transfer offices with processes and policies designed for a win–win for both the school and the large organizational partner—but some do not. If you can't find a compatible partner, don't engage.

Making University Partnership Work

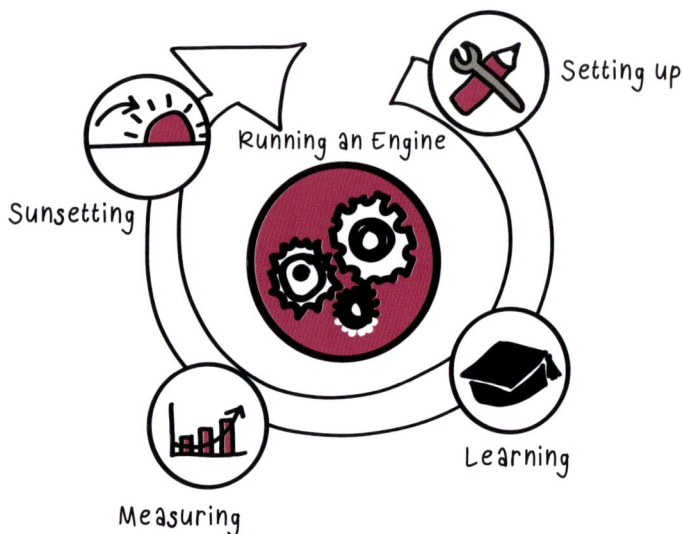

Running an Engine

Setting up

Sunsetting

Measuring

Learning

You've identified university partnership as the right next move for your company for one of, or both of, two reasons: Your company wants eyes on cutting edge research and/or your company wants access to technical/entrepreneurial talent.

Setting Up Your University Partnership[2]
CHOOSING YOUR PARTNER

Many university partnerships begin when sparks fly at a research conference or professional association gathering—university investigators share intriguing findings, and corporate innovation or research and development (R&D) leaders follow up. You can also begin your partner scan at the institutional level. If you're leaning into talent access, you'll tend to choose institutions near your HQ. If you're leaning into learning, you may want to seek the top investigators in the field, wherever they might be based—the trade-offs will be particular to your region, industry, and organization.

Note that some universities focus centrally on research vs. teaching. Your partnership falls under the research umbrella. Provided they can publish academic papers or otherwise receive tenure credit based on the research, this work is a legitimate part of the job of being a professor. Other universities require a greater teaching burden from their faculty, limiting professors' ability to participate in research. Working with more teaching-oriented universities can be done, but you might need to do something to free up faculty from required teaching time, such as providing expert staff to cover a class, or paying outright for time.

In addition to finding the right researcher(s) and locations, you'll need to assess organizational fit. Like any open innova-

tion partnership, university partnerships represent a sort of temporary marriage. You'll want to make sure your partner is someone you can live with before you exchange rings. Ask who your research and administrative partners will be, how you'll get access to lab activity and findings, what your partner will expect/require on your part. Discuss who will own what when the temporary marriage is over.

GETTING STARTED

Every university has a Technology Transfer Office (TTO) or the equivalent—a team responsible for how the university's intellectual property (IP) is shared and monetized. The TTO owns decisions about how IP is shared and what proportion of value from new findings must accrue to the university. Typically, it offers a set of standard options regarding licensing and research partnership. The TTO has many constituencies to manage: Students and faculty have different prior agreements regarding technology they might invent or help to invent. Outside partners are simultaneously sources of current revenue and sources of competition for future revenue from a joint invention. If the research includes government funding, the university has legislated rights and responsibilities to ensure the invention or findings reach the public (for example, the Bayh-Dole Act,[3] and the European Commission's open access policy[4]).

Many universities are intentionally partner-friendly and faculty-friendly as a way to sustain a thriving commercialization ecosystem. Others, perhaps inspired by relatively ancient stories of wild financial success from university inventions, claim a substantial ownership stake in new discoveries and hold a tight grip on the university's IP. The result can be that faculty are disincentivized to participate in partnerships, and the value to partners is reduced. We believe that it is a matter of time before this problematic model fades away, and all TTOs will one day be very hospitable to partners. For now, it's wise to learn about your partner's TTO's positions before you engage. To understand these positions, review public documents (for example, the University of Central Michigan publishes their

Guide to Tech Transfer[5]) and ask lots of questions such as:

- Who will manage the relationship on the administrative side, and what are their expectations?
- How are faculty incentivized to participate? Will they own part of any discoveries? Will their work with us count toward tenure?
- How does the particular faculty member want to participate in discoveries? Do they want to start a company or do they want to remain in a research role?
- What is the range of possibilities for sharing ownership of IP?
- What kinds of partnerships do you offer? Are you open to novel types?
- Are you open to our firm hiring university talent as consultants, shared part-time staff, or full-time hires? What, if any, constraints do we need to know about?
- How will university discoveries be shared with us?

TYPES OF UNIVERSITY PARTNERSHIPS

Partnerships range from low-ticket, low-touch experiences such as a research grant, to deep, high-price, high-value collaborations such as joint ventures. Consider the following options, that progress on a scale from low-touch and standardized to high-touch and bespoke.

Licensing or purchasing a university's existing IP is one way to access the near-edge of new discovery. University inventions that are sufficiently mature for patenting may be available for temporary, limited licensing, or for sale. The process for licensing is well understood and chances are your university partner already has a solid agreement framework.

Another relatively inexpensive approach is to offer *research grants*, which are simply cash given (through the university) to a professor, who uses it to conduct research. The professor may or may not be obligated to report findings back to the corporate partner, depending on prior arrangement commensurate with the fee. Research support on this scale might also be offered as a gift, with no particular expectations.

Innovation training is yet another option. In the last few decades, universities have played a crucial role in training corporate personnel to innovate. The d-School at Stanford University, Duke Corporate Education, and the Incubator for Good at the Claremont Graduate University come to mind as we write.

In-kind support means that the firm provides crucial ingredients for research, such as a dataset (be sure you have clean rights to share the data), a material, or specialized equipment—these types of resources can be invaluable to university researchers, and the research they conduct can be invaluable to the firm.

Sponsorship, as a form of partnership, covers a range of activities in which the firm pays up front and the university provides research findings back to the firm over time.

Collaborative research works like a hybrid lab, with some lab members located at the university and some at the firm, with regular communication and interdependent work.

In a *joint partnership*, the large firm and the university are true partners, creating something new together, side by side. This collaboration might be designed to drive toward new cutting-edge research, or focus on translation of existing findings. Historically, the Massachusetts Institute of Technology's (MIT) Media Lab was a classic example of a university-based home for joint partnerships.

An *applied research institute* focuses on the translation of research findings into practical tools, products, and services. Often stimulated by national/state-level priorities and partially funded by governments, applied research institutes convene and leverage government, corporate, university, and other entities.

Staffing arrangements are possible as well—you can hire a faculty member as a consultant. You can sponsor a sabbatical that pulls an investigator onto your site full time for a semester or a year. You can place a staff member onsite in a university lab.

University partnerships can be run through a *third party*, such as MagCorp,[6] a center that draws resources from Florida State University, a US national lab (the National High Magnetic Field Laboratory [MagLab]), and paying corporate partners.

Some universities go so far as to take responsibility for leading the entire ecosystem. As respected, informed, and neutral parties, universities can curate and connect stakeholders across business, government, nonprofit/nongovernmental organizations (NGOs), and academic institutions for effective collaboration.[7]

Of course, there are many more types of university engagement, for example, attending career fairs or buying naming rights to a building—while those activities might be valuable to your organization, we won't cover them here as they are outside the scope of open innovation.

UIDP, the premiere corporate/university partnership association, recommends following a developmental journey. Start simple, such as licensing patents or offering research grants, before leaping into something like a joint partnership that requires extensive trust. If your partner wants you to meet with the university president on the first day, there is most certainly a mismatch of expectations. Keep it small to begin and let it grow.[8]

PHYSICAL PRESENCE

With the type of partnership established, now it's time to consider the physical presence. Most likely, the research is best located onsite at the university, insulated by distance from the corporate handcuffs that drove you to open innovation partnership in the first place. That said, drawing experts from the university into your physical zone could be the right move if you're hiring them as consultants. Either way, you'll want as much direct contact between university and corporate staff as your partner will tolerate for the given investment. Co-presence makes room for the serendipity and extensive conversation that are essential to breakthrough innovation.[9] Direct contact is the key: You want your staff to soak up learnings as directly as possible, and develop relationships with university investigators as a basis for further hiring or partnership.

MAKING ARRANGEMENTS

NEGOTIATING INTELLECTUAL PROPERTY

The university, by its nature, represents multiple stakeholders including the TTO, the individual investigators who will work with you directly, department administrators, students, and more. The TTO holds general strategy and policies on IP. If you're willing to conform to the models they already promote, your path to a project will be shorter. If you need special arrangements, negotiation will take time and might not work.

Your most straightforward access to IP will come through licensing existing technologies or processes, which may be available for exploration, for example, on a licensing page on the university's website. You'll have the option to purchase an exclusive or nonexclusive license through a standardized procedure. If the technology is early enough and the license is exclusive, you might be asked to participate in developing the patent.

If your intention is to collaborate with university researchers to develop new technologies or processes, you'll establish an arrangement about how IP rights will be distributed. The simplest way is for each institution to maintain ownership of its own background IP (technologies and processes you each separately already own before beginning the project), and to share foreground IP resulting from the work itself. Some universities will permit sponsors to prepay for the right to monetize foreground IP.

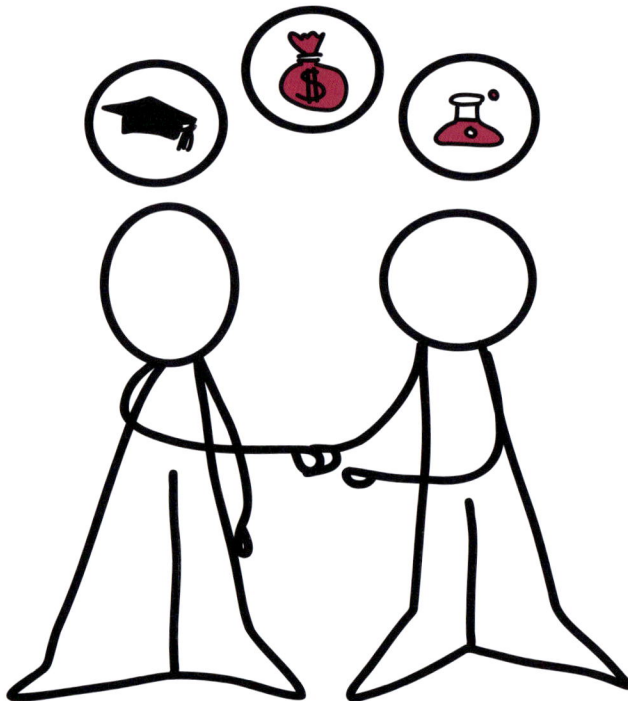

Your goal, inevitably, is commercializing. The academic investigators you'll be partnering with are primarily incentivized to publish. The goals of commercialization and publication can sit in tension with each other, so you'll need to identify projects carefully—projects that simultaneously produce commercializable knowledge and publishable papers. Develop patents together when you can. And encourage publication of ecosystem knowledge that serves your commercial goals through influence on the entire industry.

Given all of this complexity around IP, it's crucial that you develop the right internal stakeholders to inform the IP position you bring to your university partners at the start of your first engagement. Your university partnerships must align with your firm's position on IP, or you must influence your firm's position before you initiate an engagement. You don't want to encounter a serious IP obstacle in the middle of your journey.

IP is a sensitive matter for university–corporate partnerships. That said, university partnerships will rarely beat a direct path to financial success. Research results can drive important decisions long before they can turn into products. Given all of that, what if you don't care about owning the IP? What if your intention is to use the findings but not necessarily turn them directly into a product? What if the research is designed to bring adjacent industries to the place where you need them to go? What if, provided the patents are defended, you're OK with the university owning that responsibility? The odds that a particular university research project will result in something that your firm can directly commercialize are fairly low and the process is fairly slow. Furthermore, only the technology is

patentable. Any resulting insights are yours to use for future internal purposes. If you're willing to relax your IP requirements, you can move much faster and make use of valuable ideas right away.

If the projects you fund also draw on public funding, you'll need to preplan how you'll protect the IP, or preplan to share it openly. Consider sharing your findings openly in any case—you might want more science moving in your direction, even more than you want specific protection for a specific finding.[10]

NEGOTIATING FUNDING

Your costs (obviously) change with your level of engagement—the longer, more intimate, more customized, or more resource-heavy your relationship will be, the more you'll pay. A small research grant might be meaningful, even with just $10K, and you can ask for a brief report. If you're sponsoring a significant body of research, you might be looking at a six- or seven- digit commitment. Keep in mind that even these costs are likely to be lower than the cost to run an onsite engine, such as an incubator or accelerator, and much lower than the cost of an investment engine like corporate venture capital (CVC).

Note that a significant proportion, 30–70%, of your partnership fee will go to the university itself for overhead, known as indirect costs. This is standard, and is how the university covers its institutional costs, including the cost to run your partnership.

PAPERWORK

Given the relatively slow pace of decision-making on both sides of university–corporate partnership, use template agreements, wherever you can. The UIDP Contract Accords[11] offer a library of options including the project structures in the "types" section above. Once you have a few successful projects and relationships in place, a master research agreement (MRA) can provide an umbrella contract that sets the terms for multiple projects over an extended period of time.

The Minnesota Innovation Partnership (MN-IP)[12] is a well-known MRA framework that sets forth specific expectations for up-front payment, negotiated exclusivity to new IP generated from the partnership, royalties, etc.

PERSONNEL

You'll assign staff from the corporate side of the partnership, and have significant influence on the university side. In this type of partnership, especially if you are directly using it for your talent pipeline, the true collaboration is between the involved individuals.

AT THE FIRM

Assign an owner for partnerships in general, and ensure that internal staff are prepared to receive discoveries and talent opportunities that emerge.

Transfer Leader

One powerful way to maximize value from a university partnership is to place a dedicated staff person on campus to ensure that learnings and relationships accrue to the firm. For more than ten years, chemical engineer Barclay Satterfield was an innovation leader at the chemicals giant, Eastman. In her external partnerships leadership function, she held dedicated office space simultaneously at three different universities in the region around Eastman's HQ in Kingsport, Tennessee, visiting all three on a weekly basis. Her role was to oversee the transfer of knowledge and relationships between sponsored research activity occurring on each campus and staff within the firm who could benefit.

Scientist/Engineer

Staff scientists and engineers are the first line of learning from university partnerships. They may be the ones to identify relevant university investigators and technologies in the first place. They are certainly the right staff to evaluate discoveries, and the right collaborators in joint partnerships. To get maximum value from your partnerships, carve out time and provide appropriate incentives for active participation by scientists and engineers. Expect them to visit the lab, at minimum attending meetings and presentations, better yet participating directly in the research. Expect them to deliver insights and interesting talent candidates back to HQ.

Business Owners

Plan in advance for business owners to receive results from university partnerships, and engage them as deeply as you can. They'll be the ones who will decide how, and even whether, a partnership discovery influences or creates a line of business. Get their input up front, and keep them close to the work for the best chance of actually commercializing the findings in the long run. At the same time, refrain from overpromising. Results of university partnerships arrive in years rather than months. Business owners may benefit sooner from the talent pipeline the university represents, so look for opportunities to help them develop relationships with potential future hires.

AT THE UNIVERSITY

For some models, you'll pursue relationships with specific faculty. For others, the university itself will help you find matches.

Faculty

Generally, the principal investigator (PI) in any given lab is a faculty member who has secured enough resources from grants, sponsorships, and the university itself to fund a lab along with necessary equipment, lab managers and operational staff, and additional researchers (usually post-docs and graduate students). University faculty are extremely entrepreneurial in the sense that their career depends on carving out an area of research and making brand-new discoveries. They usually have teaching and/or administrative responsibilities, but when it comes to research, they have no real boss and are given no research assignments. They make their own research decisions about what to study and how to study it, while

operating under intense funding pressure. In these behaviors they are somewhat similar to startup founders. However, they are typically not business people and may have little interest in business—their career trajectory and their ability to raise grant money are driven by publication of new findings, not by commercializing anything. These motives are very different from yours, but can be complementary if you structure the project correctly. The discoveries that faculty make typically belong to the university. Faculty members may be available for consulting on a full-time temporary or part-time basis. Less often, they may wish to leave the university for a corporate role. If their research has promising commercial implications, they may wish to start a company.

Students

In university partnerships, you'll encounter graduate, and sometimes undergraduate, students attached to a PI's lab. These students are paid very low wages for their work and sometimes nothing at all. Their incentive is to gather work experience and, for graduate students, complete a dissertation that is their ticket to achieving their degree. They may wish to set up papers that can help them win tenure when they become professors. Their discoveries may or may not belong to the university—it's a good idea to understand this when you're negotiating IP arrangements. Many students wish to become professors in their own right, but many do not. They will be a primary source for your talent pipeline.

Administration

The TTO or equivalent is a key counterpart—as we've described, the TTO is deeply involved in IP and financial negotiations, and owning legal activities such as licensing, patenting, and agreements. Their primary incentive is to make money for the university, and they have a range of notions about how best to do that. A flexible, creative TTO can be an excellent partner.

You may also encounter department administrators whose faculty and students are your colleagues in the partnership. Depending on department and university culture and structure, administrators may be thrilled by your presence, or may find it draining of limited resources. It's valuable to keep department administrators in your corner as positive stakeholders, so you'll want to listen to them carefully and support them where you can.

Running your University Partnership

University partnership is really an umbrella term for several different types of activities, as we've described. This diversity means your activities will be somewhat different depending on which types you choose. The good news is that, in this engine, the lion's share of the effort for running the partnership tends to lie with the university partner. Generally speaking, the university is managing the lab, identifying researchers, providing reports, etc.

As long as you've set up staff roles, such as a transfer leader, scientist/engineer, and business owners, you have a good chance of receiving and absorbing the insights and discoveries that can emerge from your university partnership. It's critical that you maintain healthy operations: Deliver resources on time, show up to collaborate in the planned way (e.g., side by side or through reporting), and collect findings. And it's critical that your transfer leader tracks these activities consistently and maintains them at a high level—you don't want to miss valuable findings or lose the social connection with your partner.

Learning from a University Partnership

Place your staff in the closest possible proximity to the university's activities, all the way to direct collaboration when you can. That's the best way to ensure your firm acquires the learning available, including publications, physical inventions, and the insights that arise day to day. If you can't achieve truly collaborative work, look for a regular cadence of information sharing. Know when you'll receive a report, when you can do a lab visit, and when you can host an event. Make sure the information gets all the way to the decision-makers who can do something with it: scientists, engineers, product teams, and business owners. And make sure their feedback gets incorporated into the partnership at the next opportunity. Note that the more you pay, the more you're likely to be entitled to proximity.

Keep in mind that one important type of learning is learning about people: Your university partnerships are a powerful source of future staff, not just ideas, technologies, and trends.

171

University Partnership

Measuring a University Partnership

As discussed, there are at least two major motives for creating university partnerships. Therefore, both should be considered when measuring the engine and its outcomes: New science and technology, and the talent pipeline.

Preparation phase metrics	Operation phase metrics	Outcome phase metrics

• Number of relevant universities identified as potential partners (this is your baseline)
• Fraction of initial discussions initiated with the universities from your potential partner list
• Fraction of contracts under consideration from the total number of universities contacted
• Time to get contract signed
	• Number of face-to-face contact opportunities between firm and university staff
	• Fraction of in-person sessions that result in a discovery, per unit of time
	• Number of direct interpersonal contacts between the firm and potential future hires
	• Satisfaction of staff involved with the partnership (e.g., net promoter score (NPS))
	• Satisfaction of university partners
		• Number of discoveries generated in a unit of time (qualitative and quantitative)
		• Impact of lessons learned along the way (qualitative and quantitative)
		• Science and technology outcomes (examples)
		  - Number of papers published per unit of time
		  - Average time from insight to published paper
		  - Number of patents generated per unit of time
		  - Average time to patent approval
		  - Quantifiable R&D impact of scientific/technological findings
		  - Quantifiable value of patents
		• Talent (examples)
		  - Number of candidates evaluated
		  - Number of offers made from the total of candidates evaluated
		  - Offers accepted
		  - Retention rate of employees coming from the university partnership
		  - Performance/value of staff acquired through the university pipeline vs. other sources

Sunsetting a University Partnership

Your agreement with the university will include clear and specific terms, so you'll know clearly when the partnership should end. Reflect, and give and receive healthy feedback. If there's anything you don't need, leave it with the partner. You might be back, so keep the bridges strong.

10
CHAPTER TEN

Consortium

Some problems are too large and require too much diverse experience and knowledge for one firm or even a pair of organizations to address, and at the same time too urgent to permit a wait-and-see approach. For problems like this, you need a consortium[1]—a group of organizations with different perspectives and expertise they can collectively bring to bear on the problem. The consortium has an enormous combined stack of capacities with which it can address a very difficult challenge. It's large enough to influence industry, for example, toward creating and adopting new standards. And the audience for its eventual solutions is huge.

Consortia are especially powerful right at the start of an emerging phenomenon, when all players are relatively uncertain about the possibilities and are thus especially susceptible to the value in working together. For example, in the early days of work on autonomous driving, we saw multiple consortia bringing together artificial intelligence (AI) researchers, robotics inventors, and the automotive industry—large and small firms, as well as universities and governments. As of this writing, in part due to the work of consortia, some of the challenges of autonomous driving are sufficiently solved that individual companies can move forward with autonomous vehicle innovation. This explains the presence of Waymo taxis in San Francisco, and semiautonomous self-driving Teslas on the freeways in Silicon Valley. However, extremely difficult problems and compelling opportunities remain in the transportation *system*, including traffic law, the behavior of nonautonomous drivers, and possibilities that open when autonomous vehicles can communicate with each other. These problems are beyond the control of any single organization, so the power of working in a consortium remains.

A single convener can launch a consortium. For example, in 2021, the US government launched a consortium to address health equity through AI.[2] This example, AIM-Ahead, also shows the potential size of consortia, with thousands of participating entities.

At the time of this writing, we are relatively early in the expansion of generative AI into ordinary use, and it's not possible to know, yet, what that means for the workforce. It's not surprising that Google, Cisco, IBM, and others launched a consortium to investigate this.[3]

For the purposes of this book, we'll be talking about consortia formed for the purpose of innovating around an industry-level blockage. There may also be entities called consortia that are formed for commercial collaboration purposes without any particular investigation question—you'll have to read a different book for that.

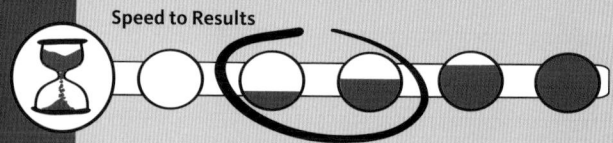

Speed to Results

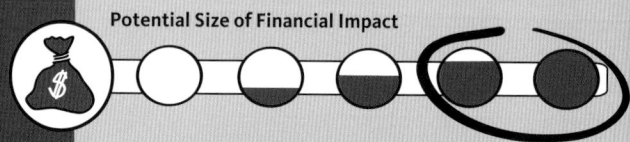

Potential Size of Financial Impact

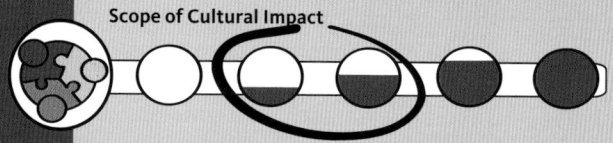

Scope of Cultural Impact

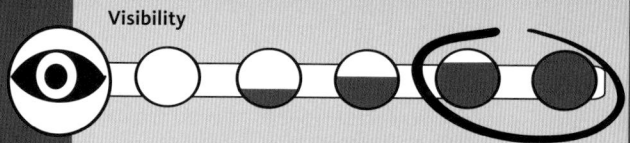

Visibility

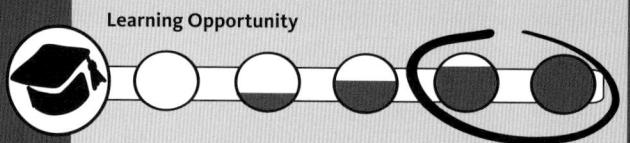

Learning Opportunity

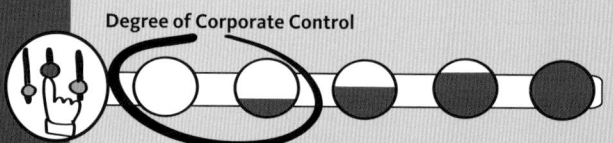

Degree of Corporate Control

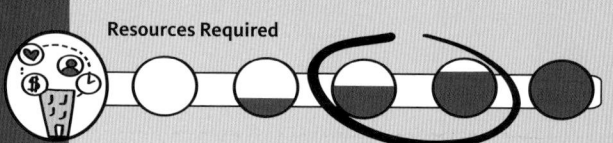

Resources Required

Demand for Speed

Potential Size of Financial Impact

Scope of Cultural Impact

Visibility

Learning Opportunity

Degree of Corporate Control

Resources Required

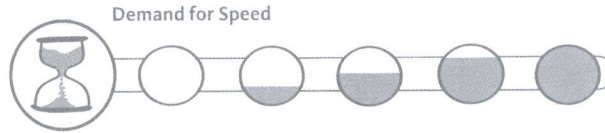

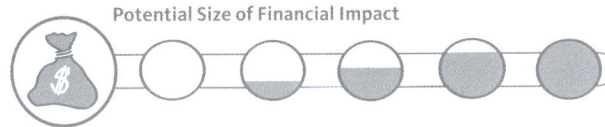

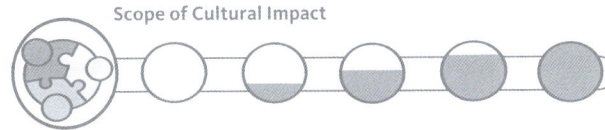

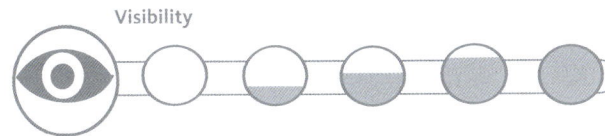

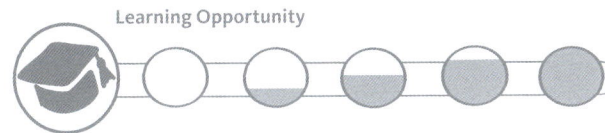

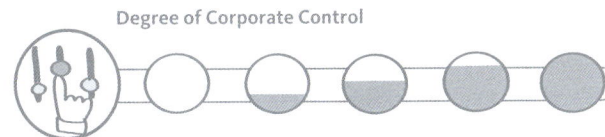

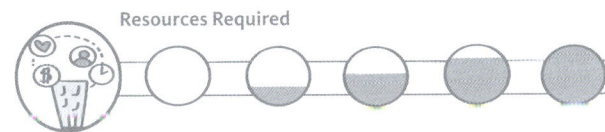

Bend the
back cover flap
over this page
to see your scales
and the Engine's scales
side by side.

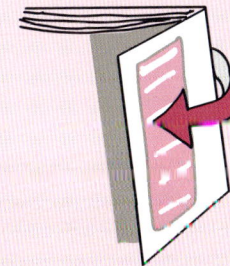

Consortium Scales

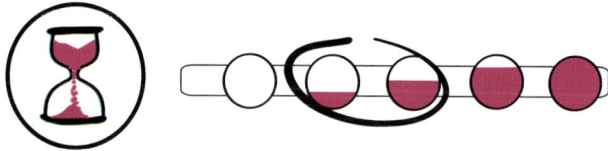

SPEED TO RESULTS:

The purpose of forming a consortium, the reason to put in the effort, is to address a difficult, important, and unsolved problem. So, you shouldn't expect results tomorrow. You'll need time for the participating entities to entwine their capacities. You can speed up the process with clear expectations and preset boundaries so that all players know what can be freely shared.

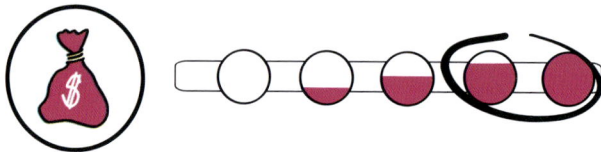

POTENTIAL SIZE OF FINANCIAL IMPACT:

The problem you're solving should have enormous impact when solved. Even shared across entities, the financial impact should be very high if all goes well.

SCOPE OF CULTURAL IMPACT:

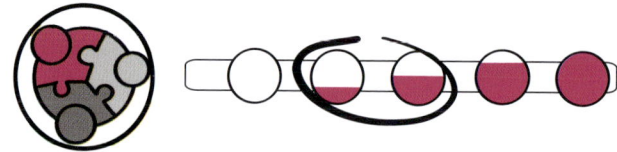

Depending on the scope of the problem and the number of your staff who need to participate in the consortium, you might see some impact on the culture.

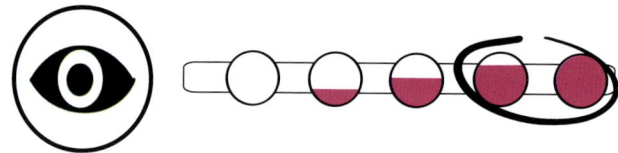

VISIBILITY:

Consortium participants make a point of publicizing their consortium work. This provides innovation credibility, as well as transparency for stakeholders.

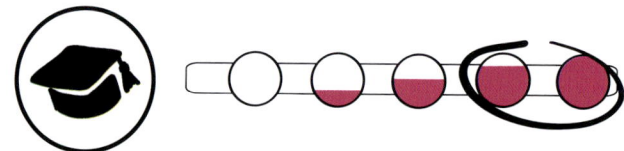

LEARNING OPPORTUNITY:

Learning is absolutely the primary purpose of the consortium. You're guaranteed to learn something significant just by trying, even if your consortium doesn't bear financial fruit in the long run.

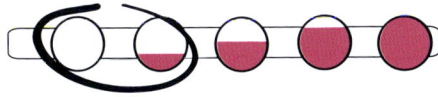

DEGREE OF CORPORATE CONTROL:

You are in control of what you bring to the consortium, and what you choose to share. You can't control what any other entity does. However, you do get a voice in designing the consortium up front, and that's where you can express your own requirements, offerings, and boundaries.

RESOURCES REQUIRED:

If you want results, you'll likely need to invest significantly, at least in terms of staff time and possibly in terms of resources, either directly to feed the consortium, or indirectly to take advantage internally of what you learn from the consortium.

Why You Should Choose this Engine

Build or join a consortium when you face an industry-level (or greater!) challenge that requires cross-disciplinary, cross-industry capacity to solve. Many such challenges involve bringing capacities together that have never before been combined. You may very well own significant assets and infrastructure, but you don't own the assets and infrastructure that need to be remixed with yours to solve the challenge. A consortium allows you to combine resources with others while maintaining your separate identity and commercial position. You should definitely join a consortium when you would otherwise miss out, or be dramatically slowed in your progress, on a large-scale challenge.

Why You Shouldn't Choose this Engine

If you're not willing to bring your experts, tools, inventions, capital, or other capacities into dialog with other entities, a consortium is not the right model for you—you'll have to catch up later, after others have learned collectively and shared their findings through publication or through developing new systems. You should also question the value of a consortium if the problem you're looking at together is not significant or not industry-wide, or it's something you could address through smaller-scale open innovation practice.

179

Consortium

Making a Consortium Work

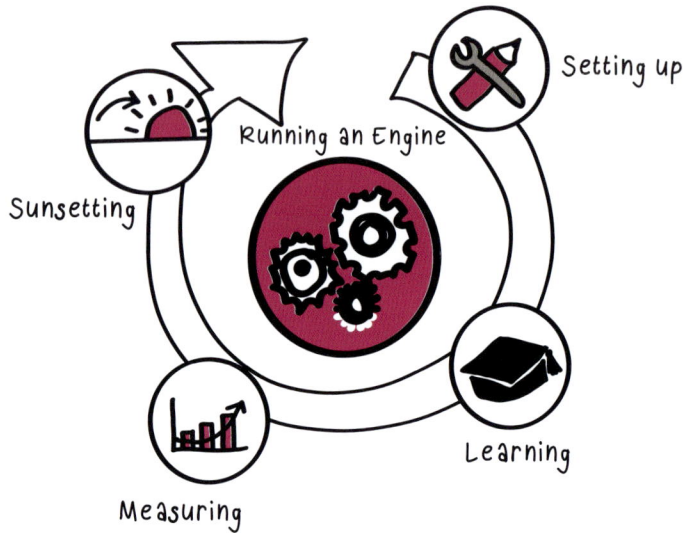

You've decided that a consortium is the best way forward for you, based on your strategic intentions, tactical commitments, and specific position. Let's assume for now that you need to create a new consortium—we'll introduce the key principles that way. If you're looking to join an existing consortium, the same principles will guide your entry.

Setting Up a Consortium

Begin setting up your consortium by defining its **mission and objectives**. The consortium must address a shared challenge or opportunity that resonates with potential participants in the given market or ecosystem. For example, the World Wide Web Consortium (W3C) was formed to develop web standards that would benefit the entire digital ecosystem.[4] A clear and compelling vision such as this ensures alignment among members and attracts diverse stakeholders.

Next, **identify your partners.** As a founding member, or perhaps *the* founding member, it's up to you to understand and recognize who needs to be at the table. A successful consortium typically involves a mix of companies, universities, research institutions, and public agencies. Diversity in expertise, resources, and perspectives fosters innovation and ensures the consortium is well-equipped to achieve its goals. For instance, the Battery500 Consortium, led by the Pacific Northwest National Laboratory,[5] brought together national labs, academia, and industry partners to develop next-generation batteries, leveraging the unique capabilities of each participant. The scale and scope of a consortium's work means that you might very well need to partner with your competitors in order to establish infrastructure, such as supply chains or standards, that will benefit all parties.

How will you attract members? You need a compelling **problem statement.** If you've zeroed in on a meaningful, consor-

tium-worthy challenge, your partners should easily see the benefits, such as reduced research and development (R&D) costs, opportunity to attack cutting-edge research by combining capacities, or industry-wide influence.

Once a clear direction is established and the potential members of the consortium identified, you will need a **governance framework** to maintain transparency, fairness, healthy resource management, and smooth day-to-day operations. This framework should include decision-making processes, leadership roles, intellectual property (IP) sharing structures, mechanisms for accountability and conflict resolution, and onboarding/offboarding procedures as firms enter and leave the consortium. Will decisions be made by consensus, supermajority, or majority? Are new members invited? If so, can anyone willing to pay the fee join, is there a selection process, or is it invitation only? Set up clarity from the start—ambiguity in these areas can lead to misunderstandings, delays, and even conflicts, undermining the group's ability to achieve its objectives. Ensure that your governance mechanisms are flexible enough to adapt to changing circumstances while remaining inclusive of diverse member perspectives. Establish how decisions are made, and where each participant's voice can have the most impact, and participants will escalate issues constructively. Depending on your goals, you may wish to operate as a temporary, informal organization, or set up a separate legal entity for a new joint institution. A nice example: the European Space Agency's Copernicus Consortium operates with a structured governance model that defines roles for member countries, ensuring equitable participation and resource allocation.[6]

Funding the consortium is a critical matter—not just the amount but how it is generated. Depending on the consortium's scope, funding may come from membership fees, public grants, or private investments. For example, take the Sematech Consortium. Originally founded to counteract Japan's significant market share in the semiconductor market, Sematech brought together semiconductor manufacturers, but relied mostly on government subsidies and industry contributions to support its early development of advanced manufacturing technologies.[7] Sematech closed its doors after more than 30 years in 2015 (for more on this, see the Sunsetting section below).

As with every other open innovation engine, thoughtful **IP management** is a must. Rules governing IP ownership, sharing, and commercialization must be established up front to prevent disputes and incentivize participation. The Linux Foundation, which facilitates open-source projects, exemplifies effective IP management. The Foundation ensures that members benefit from shared innovations while protecting proprietary contributions by providing a neutral host foundation for IP governance. This structure ensures that members can benefit from shared innovations while protecting their proprietary contributions. The foundation offers governance and community assistance, resources such as events, marketing, and training, and the ability to raise and manage funds, all within a framework that safeguards the IP of its projects and contributors.[8]

181

Prepare the **tracking mechanisms** you'll need for resource management, measurement, and accountability—these will vary depending on what you're aiming to achieve as a consortium. Include clear consequences for noncompliance. Every member has a clear stake in knowing how their resources are spent, where any obstacles lie, and what is being achieved.

If you're approached for or see opportunity in an *existing* consortium, check the same considerations: Assess whether the consortium's mission as stated truly aligns with your long-term objectives. Understand costs and commitments. Membership often involves financial contributions, resource sharing, or active participation in working groups. And, of course, you'll review the governance structures and IP policies to ensure you're on board—you'll be beholden to the frameworks that dictate decision-making and how shared innovations are managed. One last consideration as you determine whether to join an existing consortium: As a new member, do you want to help shape its direction? If so, is that opportunity available?

So—your consortium is prepared. Here's how it runs. We'll assume from here on out that you have significant leadership responsibilities.

Running a Consortium

Consortia can be vastly diverse in their size, scope, and intentions, so we won't say much about the day-to-day administration—you'll work out who needs to meet and how often, what needs to be delivered by when, and how you'll track contributions and resource utilization. Between you, this group of mature organizations should have excellent administrative capacity. Together, according to your predetermined governance model (see previous section above), you'll distribute roles across leadership positions (e.g., chairing a steering committee or working group), technical positions (e.g., scientists, engineers, financial, strategists, financial backers, etc.).

Rather than talking about the details of administration, it's important to recognize that the way individuals in the consortium lead and influence each other will be distinct from the way individuals inside a single hierarchical organization lead and influence each other. In short: Your usual carrots and sticks don't apply. Trust and leadership through influence are valuable in all circumstances—but they are essential in the context of a cross-organization consortium.

TRUST

Trust is a cornerstone. In the absence of trust, information will not be shared and a shadow of mistrust will accompany every decision. Transparency in communication, fairness in decision-making, and a shared commitment to the consortium's objectives are essential to establishing and maintaining trust.

LEADERSHIP THROUGH INFLUENCE

Within a consortium, hierarchy won't work the same way as it does inside your institution. Typically, the consortium itself employs few or no employees—all or most participants report to the member organizations. Participants are primarily beholden to their employer, not to the consortium itself, and certainly not to you. There's no opportunity to give orders, or bonuses, or to provide or remove plum opportunities. Regardless of your title, your opinion may carry no particular weight with your counterparts from partner organizations. You'll have to lead through influence.

- *Listen intently*. The whole point of working in a consortium is to pull varied perspectives together. When you find yourself disagreeing with your partner, you've struck gold! Dig into the disagreement, find out what your counterpart knows or has experienced that's driving them to an opposing position. In other words, it's an opportunity to see something you weren't able to see before, and reveal something your partner couldn't see on their own either. Unearth the heart of the difference of opinion to exploit the diverse thinking. Another crucial benefit: The act of listening makes your partner feel heard and invites deeper engagement.
- *Wield empathy*. This works in both directions: Pick up on your partner's nonverbal cues and use them to help you look at the world through your partner's eyes. And, manage your own nonverbal cueing: If you're relaxed and smiling, your partner is likely to loosen up as well. For a deeper dive into tactical empathy, we recommend *Never Split the Difference* by Chris Voss.[9]
- *Negotiate from goals, not from positions*. This core principle from the classic negotiation work, *Getting to Yes*,[10] can release you from a stuck situation and open more opportunity and more learning.
- *Third-party authority*. For reasons we don't entirely understand, sometimes it works better when someone outside the situation says exactly the same thing you're saying. If you need to persuade someone, try bringing in an outside speaker or text.

One of the greatest strengths of a consortium is its ability to drive innovation through collaboration. Create environments that encourage brainstorming, cross-disciplinary dialog, and experimentation. Establishing shared platforms for knowledge exchange ensures that ideas flow freely among members, enriching the consortium's outcomes. As a participant, be proactive in sharing insights and learning from others. Engage with working groups, attend workshops, and actively seek out opportunities to collaborate on projects. Contribute your expertise and resources while respecting the contributions of others. This reciprocity not only strengthens the consortium's output but also enhances your reputation and influence within the consortium.

Learning from a Consortium

One of the most critical aspects of joining a consortium is capturing knowledge. Participating in a consortium provides organizations with invaluable opportunities to gain knowledge, benchmark against peers, and integrate new innovations into their pipelines. The value of this learning extends beyond immediate outcomes, fostering long-term growth and adaptability.

Take, for example, the eTOX initiative kickstarted by the Innovative Medicines Initiative (IMI) consortium, which was established in 2010 to share and utilize toxicology data. This initiative aimed to create and distribute tools to predict drug side effects based on preclinical experiments. The consortium brought together twenty-five pharmaceutical companies, biotech companies, and universities, including Novartis and Bayer as coordinators, with participants such as AstraZeneca, Boehringer Ingelheim, and Pfizer. The project was funded by the IMI and had an overall estimated budget of €18.7 million.[11] Through participation in IMI projects like eTOX, pharmaceutical companies have been able to enhance their R&D productivity by accessing shared data and collaborative networks.

Benchmarking against industry peers is another key benefit of joining a consortium and a form of learning. Consortia often bring together competitors, offering rare insights into industry standards, trends, and ways of working; by comparing performance, companies can identify areas for improvement and adapt best practices.

To maximize learning, approach the idea of joining a consortium with a strategic and open mindset. You should actively

participate in working groups, seek out opportunities for collaboration, and continuously assess how the consortium's outputs align with your objectives and goals. By doing so, you ensure that your involvement not only benefits the consortium but also drives your own innovation and growth.

Measuring a Consortium

Measure the right metrics at each phase, and customize them to your context.

Preparation phase metrics	Operation phase metrics	Outcome phase metrics
• Number of organizations expressing interest in joining per unit of time • Number of formal membership applications per unit of time • Average amount of initial funding or resources pledged by each joining member	• Number of active projects or initiatives kicked off in a unit of time • Percentage of participating members contributing to active projects • Average number of meetings and workshops held per unit of time • Resource utilization efficiency metrics (e.g., members' budget burn rate) • Progress against pre-defined milestones • Number of knowledge-sharing activities conducted per unit of time	• Adoption rate of consortium outputs at member company level • New revenue or cost savings generated per unit of time or cumulative, as a result of the learnings from the consortium • IP generated per unit of time by the consortium • Technology transfer success rate at member company level • Return on investment (ROI) per participating member, comparing the costs of participation against tangible benefits gained • ROI at the consortium level, comparing the costs of the full consortium effort against consortium-level results (e.g., new industry standards, supply chains, technical solutions, etc.)

185

Consortium

Sunsetting a Consortium (or Exiting as a Member) When a consortium achieves its objectives or its relevance diminishes, it's time to sunset (or depart). For instance, the Sematech Consortium, which revolutionized semiconductor manufacturing in its early years, eventually evolved into a broader initiative before scaling down as industry needs shifted.

Plan a structured closure. Establish timelines, allocate remaining resources, and ensure the fair distribution of IP and other outputs among members.

It's critically important to document the consortium's impact. A comprehensive final report that highlights achievements, key milestones, and lessons learned ensures that the consortium's legacy endures. For instance, the closure of the Open Platform 3.0 Consortium, which focused on interoperability standards, left behind widely adopted guidelines that continue to influence the industry[12].

If you choose to leave a consortium that is continuing on without you, leave gracefully to preserve reputation and relationships. Ideally, there are exit terms in place through the governance structure, but in any case, make sure you fulfill any financial obligations and finalize commitments.

Above all, exploit the value you received from the consortium. Integrate the resulting knowledge, IP, and market insights into your operations. The time and resources invested in the consortium should yield lasting benefits, even after you leave.

Make sunsetting or exiting a consortium a productive conclusion rather than a disruptive end, paving the way for future opportunities.

CONCLUSION
Start Tomorrow

In the beginning, we told you a resonant story (Borders) about partnership and open innovation. As you progressed through the book, we've shown you how to make sense of the ecosystem around you and use it to see what partners and relationships you need. We've given you a framework (the dashboard) for understanding your internal stakeholders and setting up joint intentions. We've invited you to create an internal open innovation squad/advisory board of influential stakeholders. We've shown you how different open innovation engines work, and how they can fit your organization's maturity, capacities, and strategic needs. Before we prepare you for some key challenges and then close, sending you off to your own open innovation works, we'll lightly describe some additional, quasi-open innovation models you might have heard of. While famous, these are models we're less likely to use or recommend in practice for reasons we'll explain.

Quasi-open Innovation Engines

Several popular business practices share characteristics with open innovation—these may be valuable practices for your business, but they do not replace the crucial activity of partnering outside the organization in order to learn. These practices include mergers and acquisitions (M&A), venture building or venture studio, venture clienting, innovation competitions, innovation centers, and open innovation outsourcing.

Mergers and Acquisitions

We make a distinction between general M&A, a core business practice your firm has no doubt been engaged in for many years, and firm-altering M&A. General M&A is buying growth by adding profitable companies, buying talent by adding talent teams, or sometimes, alas, buying a promising competitor in order to shut it down (known as catch-and-kill). General M&A practice is well-known and relatively straightforward at the front end (making the purchase)—chances are your firm already employs a dedicated and highly skilled team for this work. At the back end, integration, that is, combining the new arrival into your firm, is a famously thorny problem. Cultures are different, technology systems are different, business cycles are different. In the short run, M&A can be very exciting, but in the long run it rarely works. Even when it does, our position is that M&A is typically not an innovation practice. You are buying a mature business, or you are buying a team for the purpose of adding them to your core business staff. These are valuable activities for the stability and growth of your core business. Just remember that bringing in finished ideas doesn't provide a hedge against an uncertain future. That's what we're trying to do in open innovation.

To be fair, we have seen M&A function as open innovation. M&A becomes open innovation when its goal is to drive a major pivot for the firm's strategy. The travel company, TUI, held airplanes and hotels, and saw its function as bringing travelers to their destination. TUI acquired the attraction-ticketing firm, Musement, as a way to extend its business from the hotel door into the destination locale.[1] As of this writing, Musement represents a major component of TUI's business, and the entire concept of TUI's work has changed. This kind of transformative M&A can be the result of a well-executed prove-out journey.

Venture Building/Venture Studio

Starting a new business from scratch is called venture building. Spinning up a shop that focuses on venture building is called venture studio. Either can be done internally or through third-party service providers. Building new ventures internally is subject to the same structures that prevent the core business

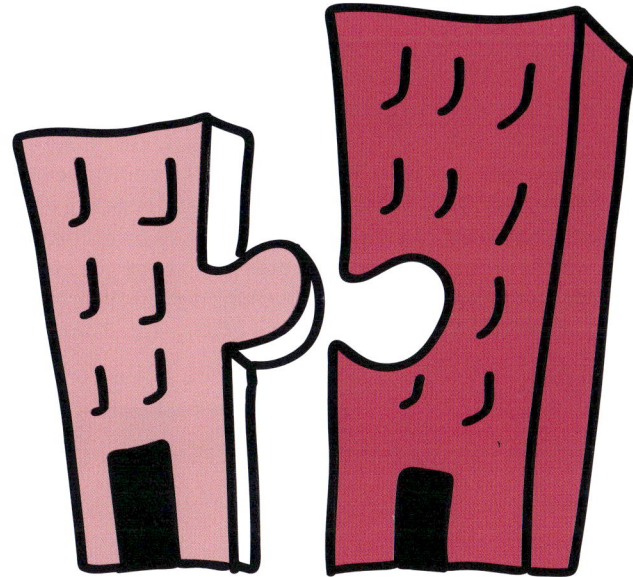

from fully exploring the future. Internal venture-building efforts are constrained by the same regulatory considerations you face in the core business, and likely the same process, legal, brand, and cultural considerations as well. You might be able to set up exceptions in some cases, but the fundamental relationship of the venture-building effort to the brand is still likely to be a barrier—there's no partner present whose gifts complement yours and allow you to do something together you can't do alone. If you spin up a separate firm to do venture building, and/or outsource the effort to a third party, you may be released from your core business constraints, but you'll still have the difficulty of integrating your new business to contend with, similar to traditional M&A. We have heard arguments that a firm should create new companies and simply take profit from them over the medium and long run, with no integration effort. We think that's an interesting idea, but we're not ready to call it open innovation unless you're truly using these new ventures as hedges against the future. You'd have to expect, and be ready, to pivot the business to whichever of these efforts works best at any given time, and we haven't seen that (yet). Some analysts think of venture building as a particularly hands-on form of corporate venture capital (CVC).

Venture Clienting

Venture clienting is simply acting as a startup's first customer. This is invaluable to startups and does absolutely support your reputation in the open innovation ecosystem. However, in practice, you're buying a finished product from a less-known vendor, not exploring the future on your own behalf, per se. Remember the Borders story? Established firm, Borders, hiring early upstart Amazon could be considered venture clienting—that one didn't go so well for the established firm. If you're going deeper, truly working with the startup to transform the product into something that helps you make sense of the future, then it's open innovation. We'd describe this practice as part of a prove-out journey—flip back to that section to learn more.

Innovation Competitions

In a typical innovation competition, a large organization issues a challenge. Startup founders and other inventors apply. A selection is made, and the winning team receives a cash prize. The large organization gets visibility for its attention to innovation and to the topic of the challenge (often related to a United Nations Sustainable Development Goal[2] such as Affordable and Clean Energy). It may also get some new ideas and a sense for what inventors are thinking about. Inventors and founders get some visibility and, if they're lucky, some cash.

On the surface, this seems like a good open innovation move. Unfortunately, we have not yet seen these challenges convert into true partnership projects where something new is generated. Normally, as soon as the prize is given, the challenge and the relationship are over. This might be in part because issuing a challenge signals a low maturity level on the part of the corporate: Why would you spend time on a challenge if you already understood the ecosystem? Applicants are also likely to represent less-mature startups—the more mature ones can't drop what they're doing to pursue a prize. All of that said, competitions can make a valuable entryway to your open innovation practice—connecting appealing applicants (whether or not they win) with a prove-out journey, accelerator, incubator, or even CVC downstream.

Innovation Centers

Where Diana lives in Silicon Valley, it's common to see large firms set up a physical location and name it an innovation center or technology center. These are often designed as a way to showcase internal innovation to the outside world, especially potential customers. When they are successful as open innovation engines, they are essentially operating as physical sites for prove-out journeys. If you build a prove-out journey engine and need a special physical site (e.g., to work with large, dangerous, or fragile materials), why not call it an innovation center and use it for visibility—that seems like a good idea! We've covered what we think would be most important in the prove-out journey chapter.

Open Innovation Outsourcing

It is entirely possible to outsource open innovation to third parties. Our perspective is that large organizations should be deeply involved in open innovation efforts in order to catch and integrate the insights and technologies that emerge. Using a third party can be a great way to get started with open innovation efforts—that said, we strongly recommend that you plan from the start to spin your open innovation engine *in,* within two years. Otherwise, your expensive experience will disappear with your vendor. You're at risk of delegating understanding—the Borders story and the Eames' (see What is Open Innovation at the start of the book) have told us never to do that!

Do by all means engage in M&A, build new ventures, and buy from startups—these are healthy aspects of normal business growth and scale. By all means attract attention with competitions, this could be a useful marketing practice. Just keep in mind that you'll need one or more of the main engines we've described if you're serious about mitigating, or better yet leading, the future through open innovation.

Facing Challenges

You're about to embark on a new journey. Before you start, we'd like to share two challenges we've seen in the field—be aware so you can handle them before they slow you down.

CHALLENGE: ADDRESSING CORPORATE "ANTIBODIES"

Have you heard of this term? It's a favorite among innovation consultants—and it's an apt metaphor: Like a human body, your firm feels healthiest when things are stable. Like a human body, your firm has something like an immune system to protect it from disruption. Usually, when we hear people talk about "antibodies," the speakers are change-makers expressing frustration with the system for rejecting their change.

We like to point out that stability is a good thing! The corporate immune system helps ensure everyone's regular paycheck, including the paychecks for the innovation team. Since some changes are important, you'll need to find a way through them. So let's talk about how to recognize "antibodies," how to address them, and when necessary, how to work around them.

We consistently see two types of antibodies: Financial antibodies and social antibodies.

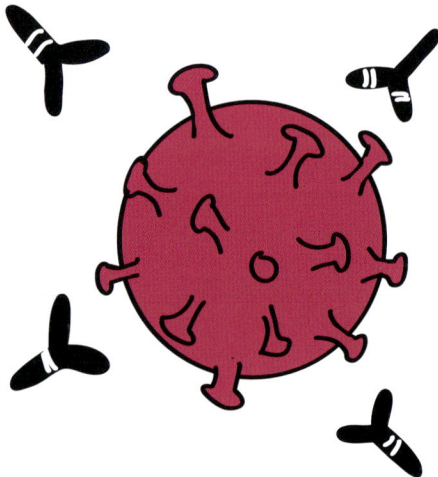

Financial Antibodies

Money is an important mode of expression for your firm's immune system. Your firm's standard processes include scrutiny as money comes in through your project funding and as any financial results appear on the other side.

- **Fund Open Innovation as a Standard Business Practice Rather than a Fixed Asset**

Typically, open innovation efforts are funded as capital expenses, as if they were buildings or large machines that arrive on the books mainly as a one-time, up-front expense. If your firm funds open innovation as if it's a factory, you'll have to measure its success as if it's a factory, delivering known products to a known audience at a known time. It's easy to say no to building another factory.

Ideally, you want your open innovation effort to be funded as an operational, ongoing expense—the practice of open innovation should continue forward at all times, even as you update and switch between engines based on results and strategy. Ending your open innovation effort should feel like ending your marketing efforts: Unthinkable! You'll have to show metrics, like marketing does. And your decisions won't always be perfectly tied to income, like marketing's efforts (what is the value of a billboard, for example?).

If you can, as soon as you can, make the case that open innovation should be a normal part of doing business.

- **Call on Other Departments to Measure Their Invisible Externalities**

If your work is perceived as competing with core business product lines for resources, you're up against a serious challenge. In many organizations, the core business gets its new products "for free" from the efforts of the research and development (R&D) department. There is no particular internal accounting that shows that the organization paid via R&D effort for its products. The product organization gets to claim revenue without having to offset it with this critical and very costly expense.[3]

In the case of the open innovation team, whose discoveries come from external sources, your expenses will be fully visible. Level the playing field when you share metrics. Set the cost of open innovation investigation in context: Side by side with the cost of R&D and internal innovation.

Social Antibodies

The human beings in your firm are incentivized to protect the familiar. Consider adjusting your incentive systems to encourage an appetite for change, especially for frontline leaders. And note that some folks may just not want change to happen—give them room.

- **Support Managers**

The dashboard process, and just about every open innovation engine, requires input from frontline staff—engineers, scientists, designers, business model specialists, etc. The more exciting your work, the more these frontline staff are likely to want to participate. Their efforts represent a cost that is paid by one class of employee: Frontline managers. Chances are these managers get no help when their staff are pulled into your efforts—no help, no recognition, no compensation, they're simply expected to make do with less than the already scant budget they start with. Think about what you can do to make them feel like it matters. Think about how you can recognize them, bonus them, and back up their resources. In essence, use your actions and words to convert them to allies and let them make change on your behalf.

- **Give a Wide Berth to People Who Don't Want What You're Bringing**

People whose work might be disrupted by your efforts may end up being your greatest allies (if they know they need to peer into the future), or your worst enemies (if they are attached to the status quo). The change writer, Greg Satell, recommends leaving the likely saboteurs out of any discussions until the deed is just about done."

CHALLENGE: ADDRESSING LOCAL CONTEXT

You might be working in a place we've never visited and couldn't find on a map. Your region might not have much ecosystem activity yet, or your ecosystem might look very different from the examples we've given. Your specific context might make it much harder to meet people or to collaborate in the ways we've described. If that's the case, take what you've read here and apply the principles to your own circumstances. As one of our former co-authors once said: "*Principles are universal. Tactics are contextual.*"[5]

So, what are the principles? Everywhere, large organizations have natural, as well as regulatory, constraints that limit their ability to probe the future. Partnership with other entities with different, complementary challenges and superpowers (in other words, open innovation), makes sense as an ongoing practice. Internal alignment, as with the Open Innovation Dashboard, is a requirement for effective partnership. It's wise to match your organization's positioning with what partners bring to the table. Partnerships need preparation, operation, and measurement. With those principles in mind, how are you going to go about executing on the tactics?

With those principles in mind, what will you create where you are?

Open Innovation is Imperative

We started writing this book because we were concerned that many organizations were unprepared for the pace of change in the business environment at that time. We have seen many organizations attempt to expand from internal innovation to open innovation with a limited understanding of what open innovation entails. Our intention with this book is to launch companies into open innovation, free of the traditional mistakes they have historically made in internal innovation.

Just in the short time since then, the pace of change has increased dramatically. It's no longer credible to deny it. Your organization needs a designated, operating function whose job it is to make sense of change through participation in change, and to mitigate for, or better yet lead, change. The term "innovation" may be inadequate for the job, but it's the one we have at this moment. This medium- and long-term contingency planning should no longer be considered optional.

Working with others outside your organization is a fundamental pillar of making sense of the future. No matter how brilliant your scientists, engineers, and business leaders are, they are constrained by the operating model of your organization: The structures, culture, and processes that define the organization also serve to focus its energy and transform it from a bunch of people into a cruising battleship. You can't remove the frame or your organization will sink. But you must send probes outside the frame or your organization will run aground. Open innovation provides your portholes, your spyglass, your sonar, your periscope, and your grappling hooks.

As we write, the pace of change driven by large language models (LLMs) alone is incredible, and it's likely there will be another change-force rising before you read. Now is the second-best time to start investigating your future through open innovation engines of the kinds we've described. (The best time, according to the proverb, was twenty years ago.)
.
This practice may be new for your organization, but you have relevant capacities. Chances are you already have an active M&A group with an active scouting function. Chances are you already have some product owners who are engaging outside the organization on their own time because they've smelled the future coming. At this moment in history, chances are your board members are concerned about the pace of change as well.

One crucial muscle to develop is your *absorptive capacity*.[6] How are you probing the world? How are you receiving information and technologies? How are you transforming based on what you receive? In this book, we've given you, above all, an absorptive capacity toolkit: We've talked about how to understand and engage in your ecosystem, align your organization up front (the dashboard), choose the right engines so that you're probing your ecosystem in a way that works for you, and how to build, measure, and receive ongoing value from those probes. Set up your organization to derive maximum learning value and material value out of every exploration and engagement.

And now, we recommend you stop reading, stop analyzing, and get started. Deepen your presence in your ecosystem and run small experiments in parallel with your dashboard-based alignment work—each of those lines of effort can serve to improve the other. If you've got a board that's excited about one particular engine, take advantage of that energy to move forward. As in all innovation efforts, the learning happens when you get into the field with prototypes, and if you look at it the right way, everything's a prototype. Start in the imperfect present, use your engagement in the world to learn, and move toward something better. Treat your ecosystem map and your dashboard as living documents and use them to move you forward as you create relationships, insights, and new value.

At the start, we told you that open innovation can't solve your inherent innovation problems. What it might do, is provide you with a proof-of-concept of how innovation can work effectively. Working with outside partners, who have their own constraints, needs, desires, and limitations, can act as a forcing function to improve your absorptive capacity across the organization, including internal innovation activity. Can you take the practices you develop through open innovation and use them to reset your growth?

Notes

Part One

What Is Open Innovation and Why Does it Matter?

1. Noguchi, Y. (2011, July 19). Why Borders failed while Barnes & Noble survived. NPR. Retrieved from https://www.npr.org/2011/07/19/138514209/why-borders-failed-while-barnes-and-noble-survived

2. Raff, D.M.G. (2000). Superstores and the evolution of firm capabilities in American bookselling. *Strategic Management Journal*, 21(10/11), 1043–1059. http://www.jstor.org/stable/3094426

3. Eames: The Architect and the Painter (2011). [Film]. Quest Productions, Bread and Butter Films.

4. PitchBook. (2020, December 10). CVC sea change: Corporate venture on the rise. *PitchBook*. Retrieved from https://pitchbook.com/newsletter/cvc-sea-change-corporate-venture-on-the-rise-Hbo

5. CB Insights (2021, March 15). State of CVC Global 2021, Global data and analysis on CVC private market dealmaking, funding and exits. *CB Insights*. Retrieved from https://www.cbinsights.com/research/report/corporate-venture-capital-trends-2021/

6. Many, many works in open innovation, including the seminal book: Chesbrough, H. (2003). *Open Innovation: The New Imperative for Creating and Profiting from Technology*. Harvard Business School Press, Boston.

7. Kortoglu, T. (2023). HP's Chief Engineer, Chandrakant D.Patel, PE Patel, and I sat down to discuss open innovation. [Video]. Retrieved from https://www.linkedin.com/feed/update/urn:li:activity:6991818317976010753/

8. Viki, T., Toma, D., & Gons, E. (2017). *The Corporate Startup: How Established Companies Can Develop Successful Innovation Ecosystems*. Vakmedianet, Amsterdam. https://thecorporatestartupbook.com/

9. Toma, D., & Gons, E. (2021). *Innovation Accounting: A Practical Guide for Measuring Your Innovation Ecosystem's Performance*. BIS Publishers, Amsterdam. https://innovationaccountingbook.com

10. https://www.usace.army.mil/Business-With-Us/Partnering/mod/129895/details/443/

How Does an Open Innovation Ecosystem Work?

1. For example, https://makepossible.cmu.edu/argo-ai/

2. Joseph, D., Windham-Bannister, S., & Mangold, M. (2021). What corporates can do to help an innovation ecosystem thrive—and why they should do it. *Journal of Commercial Biotechnology*, 26(1), 3. https://doi.org/10.5912/jcb975

3. https://www.masslifesciences.com/

4. https://alliancesocal.org/

5. Fayard, A-L. & Mendola, M. (2024, April 19). The 3-stage process that makes universities prime innovators. *Harvard Business Review*. Retrieved from https://hbr.org/2024/04/the-3-stage-process-that-makes-universities-prime-innovators

6. https://lalifescience.org/resources-map/

The Open Innovation Dashboard

1. InnoLead. (2022, December 6). Successful startup engagement and corporate venture capital. InnoLead. Retrieved from https://www.innovationleader.com/research-reports/startup-engagement-corporate-venture-capital/

2. Boni, A.A., & Joseph, D. (2018). Aligning the corporation for transformative innovation: Introducing innovation dashboard 2.0. *Journal of Commercial Biotechnology*, 24(4), 14–22. Retrieved from https://corporateacceleratorforum.com/wp-content/uploads/2023/01/910-Article-Text-2606-1-10-20190906-Boni-Joseph-Dashboard.pdf

3. Kaplan, R.S., & Norton, D.P. (1996). *The Balanced Scorecard: Translating Strategy into Action*. Harvard Business School Press, Boston.

4. Viki, T., Toma, D., & Gons, E. (2017). *The Corporate Startup: How Established Companies Can Develop Successful Innovation Ecosystems*. Vakmedianet, Amsterdam. https://thecorporatestartupbook.com/

Part Two

Startup Accelerator
1. Cohen, S., Fehder, D. C., Hochberg, Y. V., & Murray, F. (2019). The design of startup accelerators. *Research Policy, 48*(7), 102378. https://doi.org/10.1016/j.respol.2019.04.003

2. https://www.nasa.gov/directorates/somd/space-communications-navigation-program/technology-readiness-levels/

3. http://www.dodmrl.com/MRL_Deskbook_2022_20221001_Final.pdf

4. Find the visualization at https://www.researchgate.net/figure/Illustration-of-the-Manufacturing-Readiness-Levels-MRLs-Level-1-denotes-a-technology_fig6_342937203. The visualization is drawn from Petrovic, S., & Hossain, E. (2020). Development of a Novel Technological Readiness Assessment Tool for Fuel Cell Technology. *IEEE Access*, 8, 132237–132252. https://doi.org/10.1109/ACCESS.2020.3009193

Startup Incubator
1. https://jnjinnovation.com/jlabs

Corporate Venture Capital
1. Thiel, P., Masters, B. (2015). Zero to One: Notes on Startups, Or how to Build the Future. United Kingdom: Virgin Books.

2. Bracy, C. (2025). The World Eaters., United States. Dutton.

3. State of CVC 2024: A Deep Dive into the Dynamics of the Corporate Venture Capital (CVC) Ecosystem. First-Citizens Bank and Trust Company. Retrieved from https://www.svb.com/trends-insights/reports/state-of-cvc/

4. Levy, A. (2019, April 11). Alphabet's investment in Uber has multiplied by 20-fold since 2013. *CNBC*. https://www.cnbc.com/2019/04/11/alphabet-uber-investment-stake-has-gone-up-20x-since-2013.html

5. State of CVC 2024: A Deep Dive into the Dynamics of the Corporate Venture Capital (CVC) Ecosystem. First-Citizens Bank and Trust Company. Retrieved from https://www.svb.com/trends-insights/reports/state-of-cvc/

6. Larson, S. (2018, February 7). How Uber and Google went from "brothers" to enemies. *CNN Business*. https://money.cnn.com/2018/02/07/technology/waymo-uber-trial-relationship/index.html

7. Gutnick, R. (2024, February 8). Corporations launched 83 venture capital funds in 2023. *Medium*. https://medium.com/touchdownvc/corporations-launched-83-venture-capital-funds-in-2023-c04e137b9131

8. Intel (2020, May 12). Intel Capital invests $132 million in 11 disruptive technology startups. *Intel Newsroom*. https://www.intc.com/news-events/press-releases/detail/1074/intel-capital-invests-132-million-in-11-disruptive

9. Strebulaev, I. and Wang, A. (2024). *Steer Clear of Corporate Venture Capital Pitfalls.* MIT Sloan Management Review.

10. Mawson, J. (2023, March 13) CVC takes a larger role in corporate innovation spend. Global Corporate Venturing. https://globalventuring.com/corporate/cvc-proportion-corporate-innovation-spend/

11. Press, G. (2019, June 18). What corporate VCs can learn from the first decade of Intel Capital. *Forbes*. https://www.forbes.com/sites/gilpress/2019/06/18/what-corporate-vcs-can-learn-from-the-first-decade-of-intel-capital/

12. Founder Institute. (2020, June 24). Template for creating a VC investment thesis. *Founder Institute*. https://fi.co/insight/template-for-creating-a-vc-investment-thesis

13. Moore, K. (2023, July 24). CVC compensation. Global Corporate Venturing. https://globalventuring.com/corporate/best-practice/cvc-compensation/

14. Chen, J. (2024, July 2) Carried interest explained: who it benefits and how it works. *Investopedia*. https://www.investopedia.com/terms/c/carriedinterest.asp

15. Arrington, L. (2023). Most CVCs invest from the balance sheet but models range from ad hoc to near-independent. Global Corporate Venturing. https://globalventuring.com/corporate/corporates-invest-from-the-balance-sheet/

16. Intel. (2025, January 14). Intel Capital to become standalone investment fund. *Intel.* https://newsroom.intel.com/corporate/intel-news-jan-2025

17. https://alliancernm.com/home-alliance/alliance-ventures/

18. The Carta Team. (2024, August 9). Convertible securities. Carta. https://carta.com/learn/startups/fundraising/convertible-securities/

19. Jacobsohn, S. (n.d.). Here's a look inside a typical VC's pipeline: A must-read for entrepreneurs. *VentureBeat*. https://venturebeat.com/entrepreneur/heres-a-look-inside-a-typical-vcs-pipeline-a-must-read-for-entrepreneurs/

20. https://www.nasa.gov/directorates/somd/space-communications-navigation-program/technology-readiness-levels/

21. Press, G. (2019, June 18). What corporate VCs can learn from the first decade of Intel Capital. *Forbes*. https://www.forbes.com/sites/gilpress/2019/06/18/what-corporate-vcs-can-learn-from-the-first-decade-of-intel-capital/

Prove-out Journey

1. Rampton, J. (2015, April 14). Why VCs don't sign NDAs (and why you shouldn't worry about it). *Entrepreneur*. https://www.entrepreneur.com/starting-a-business/why-vcs-dont-sign-ndas-and-you-shouldnt-worry-about-it/245023

2. activate.org/sipa

3. https://www.techtransfer.nih.gov/sites/default/files/documents/pdfs/slaform.pdf

4. United States Patent and Trademark Office (n.d.). MPEP S2156 Joint research agreements.. USPTO. https://www.uspto.gov/web/offices/pac/mpep/s2156.html

University Partnership

1. Fayard, A., & Mendola, M. (2024, April 19). The 3-stage process that makes universities prime innovators. *Harvard Business Review*. https://hbr.org/2024/04/the-3-stage-process-that-makes-universities-prime-innovators

2. Recommend https://uidp.org/

3. National Institute of Standards and Technology (n.d.). Bayh-Dole Act. NIST. https://www.nist.gov/tpo/policy-coordination/bayh-dole-act

4. European Commission (n.d.). Open access. European Commission. https://research-and-innovation.ec.europa.eu/strategy/strategy-research-and-innovation/our-digital-future/open-science/open-access_en

5. https://www.cmich.edu/docs/default-source/academic-affairs-division/research-and-graduate-studies/sponsored-programs/technology-transfer-and-commercialization/cmu-inventor-s-guide-june-20201f8ece78-a954-4ac2-bcc9-c974375f9f4d.pdf?sfvrsn=94051c75_3

6. https://magneticscorp.com/

7. Fayard, A., & Mendola, M. (2024, April 19). The 3-stage process that makes universities prime innovators. *Harvard Business Review*. https://hbr.org/2024/04/the-3-stage-process-that-makes-universities-prime-innovators

8. Tony Boccanfuso interview with Diana Joseph, July 2024

9. UIDP (2023, December 12). Coincidence as catalyst: The nexus of serendipity, collaboration, and productivity in U-I partnerships. UIDP. https://uidp.org/coincidence-as-catalyst-the-nexus-of-serendipity-collaboration-and-productivity-in-u-i-partnerships/

10. UIDP (2023, July 17). Balancing and assessing open access with U-I partnerships in mind. UIDP. https://uidp.org/balancing-and-assessing-open-access-with-u-i-partnerships-in-mind/

11. UIDP (n.d.). Contract accords: Guiding principles on 17 aspects of industry sponsored research agreements. UIDP. https://uidp.org/publication/contract-accords-2020/

12. University of Minnesota. (n.d.) MN-IP: Sponsoring research & innovation partnerships. University of Minnesota. https://research.umn.edu/units/techcomm/corporate-engagement/sponsoring-research-mn-ip

Consortium

1. Boni, A.A., & Joseph, D. (2019). Four models for corporate transformative, open innovation. *Journal of Commercial Biotechnology*, *24*(4).

2. https://www.aim-ahead.net

3. IBM (2024, April 4). Leading companies launch consortium to address AI's impact on the technology workforce. *IBM Newsroom*. https://newsroom.ibm.com/2024-04-04-Leading-Companies-Launch-Consortium-to-Address-AIs-Impact-on-the-Technology-Workforce

4. https://www.w3.org/mission/

5. https://www.pnnl.gov/innovation-center-battery500-consortium

6. https://www.esa.int/Applications/Observing_the_Earth/Copernicus/Introducing_Copernicus

7. U.S. Government Accountability Office (1992). *A report to Congress: The role of information technology in the economy* (GAO-RCED-92-283). U.S. GAO. https://www.gao.gov/assets/rced-92-283.pdf

8. The Linux Foundation (n.d.). Why host your project at Linux Foundation? The Linux Foundation. https://www.linuxfoundation.org/hubfs/Why%20Host%20a%20Project.pdf

9. Voss, C., & Raz, T. (2017). *Never Split the Difference: Negotiating as if Your Life Depended On It*. Random House Business Books, New York.

10. Fisher, R., & Ury, W. (1981). *Getting to Yes: Negotiating Agreement Without Giving In*. Houghton Mifflin, Boston, MA.

11. https://etoxproject.eu/

12. http://www.opengroup.org/openplat-form3.0/op3-snapshot/index.htm. Note this link may not be accessible in your region.

Start Tomorrow

1. Tolentino, T. (2018, September 17). Tours and activities M&A continues as TUI Group acquires tech start-up Musement. *Travel Daily Media*. https://www.traveldailymedia.com/tui-group-acquires-musement/

2. https://www.un.org/en/common-agen-da/sustainable-development-goals

3. Our thanks to an anonymous speaker for sharing this insight at Diana's Fireside Chat series, Click: the Startup Accelerator for Corporate Partnership. https://www.corporateacceleratorforum.com/click

4. Satell, G. (2019). *Cascades: How to Create a Movement that Drives Transformational Change*. McGraw Hill, New York.

5. Tendayi Viki, over dinner.

6. Cohen, W.M., & Levinthal, D.A. (2000). Absorptive capacity: A new perspective on learning and innovation. In Cross, R., & Israelit, S. (eds.) *Strategic Learning in A Knowledge Economy: Individual, Collective, and Organizational Learning Process*. Routledge, London. https://www.taylorfrancis.com/chapters/edit/10.4324/9780080517889-chapter3/absorptive-capacity-new-perspective-learning-innovation-wesely-cohen-daniel-levinthal

Acknowledgments

These folks provided inspiration, insight, education, comfort, and support.

We're eternally grateful.

Darren Adams
Kim Arnone
Hans Balmaekers
Ed Barker
Anna Belova
Tony Boccanfuso
Jesus Checa Caballero
Doreen Cadieux
Amanda Cashin
Melanie Colburn
Corentin Cremet
Bob Czechowicz
Nikhil Gargeya
Fernando Gomez-Baquero
Tarun Gulati
Lisa Gus
Lorin Hamlin

Geof Hannigan
Chris Haskell
Nathan Horner
Frank Hysa
Alaine Joseph
Keith Joseph
Arthur Jue
Satyam Kantamneni
Andrea Kates
Dan Kihanya
Scott Kirsner
Patricia Kroondijk
Navin Kunde
Ben Loh
Ezra Loh
Sylvie Loh
Dr. Yvonne Lutsch

Simon Maechling
Mikel Mangold
Sandy Mau
Kevin McCreight
Hunter McDaniels
Shuman Mitra
Martha Montoya
Felipe Negritto
Thomas Neubert
Michael Nichols
Grace Oliver
Paul Orlando
Tulsi Patel
Kyra Peyton
Ryan Pletka
Margarita Quihuis
Lara Ramdin

Greg Satell
David Smith
Jonathan Speed
Erin Spring
Linda Booth Sweeney
Jonathan Tan
Carroll Thomas
Jeremy Tole
Tendayi Viki
Jeannine Walsh
Sue Windham-Bannister
Bill Wishon
Mary Yang
Michele Zilli

Index

205

206